REMEMBER THE
FUTURE

REMEMBER THE
FUTURE

Financial Leadership
and Asset Management
for Congregations

GERALD W. KEUCHER

Church Publishing
NEW YORK

Church Publishing, 445 Fifth Avenue, New York, NY 10016

Church Publishing is an imprint of Church Publishing Incorporated.

Library of Congress Cataloging-in-Publication Data
Keucher, Gerald W.
     Remember the future : financial and asset management for congregations / Gerald W. Keucher.
       p. cm.
     ISBN 0-89869-518-X
     1. Church finance. 2. Episcopal Church—Finance.   I. Title
BV770.K48 2006
254'.8—dc22   2006000469

With love and gratitude to

MOTHER

Patience and abnegation of self, and devotion to others...
— Henry Wadsworth Longfellow, *Evangeline*

and

JOHN

Whose name will I call out, when death calls mine?
It will be yours — and that will be the sign.
— Gloria Maxson, "Anniversary"

Contents

Acknowledgments

This book began as a series of articles in the *Episcopal New Yorker,* the newspaper of the Episcopal Diocese of New York. The thought was that I as the controller might write "something about money." Perhaps they got more than they bargained for: the series ran for about two years. When Joan Castagnone, then an editor with Church Publishing, Inc., noticed one of the articles in the summer of 2004, she saw the possibility of a book and encouraged me to make a proposal. I'm especially grateful to Frank Tedeschi of Church Publishing, a friend of long standing, who was my editor. It has been a pleasure to work with him and with the staff of Church Publishing. Whatever is lacking in the pages that follow is my responsibility, not theirs.

I am also very thankful to others who have read the manuscript and suggested many things that made it stronger: the Reverend Deacon Claudia M. Wilson, the Reverend Lucia K. Lloyd, the Reverend Dr. Richard Sloan, Susan Fowler, and Laurie Hammel. I thank Bruce English for providing many of the numbers behind some of the discussion in chapter 3. I'm grateful to Victor Stanwick for helping with the charts and other visual aids.

I would never have been in a position to write the articles or the book if I hadn't had the privilege of working on the diocesan staff in New York, first for Canon Michael J. McPherson, formerly the controller and chief administrative officer under the Right Reverend Richard Grein, the previous bishop of New York. It is not possible to acknowledge adequately my debt to Michael, both personally and professionally, but I deeply appreciate this opportunity to try. Michael always said that the only purpose of a diocesan staff is to serve the bishops and the congregations of the diocese. That straightforward insight has provided the rod by which I have been able to measure any activity the controller's office has contemplated. Much else that I learned from Michael is also always with me.

I have been fortunate to be able to continue my work serving the Right Reverend Mark S. Sisk, the current bishop of New York. And I gratefully recognize how generous Dr. Dall W. Forsythe, who succeeded Michael as chief administrative officer, was in every possible way during his tenure. It has been gratifying to work with both of them and with the rest of the diocesan staff, an impressive group of professionals whose collegiality means much to me. I thank Michael Rebic, an expert on the maintenance and restoration of historic buildings and the director of our Property Support office, both for teaching me over the years virtually everything in chapter 4 and for assisting me in many ways with the manuscript, especially the structure of chapter 6. The Reverend Canon Andrew Dietsche's droll cartoons for each chapter are sure to make the point with memorable wit. And Carol O'Neale, the indispensable assistant controller, has made life possible since she arrived.

The Reverend Canon James Elliott Lindsley's history of the Diocese of New York, *This Planted Vine* (New York: Harper & Row, 1984), is a volume to which I return more often than any other save the Bible and the Prayer Book. I welcome this opportunity to thank him for the historical context that has meant so much to me in my work over the years. My debt is evident on many of the pages that follow.

A part of my work is supporting the Diocesan Trustees, the Diocesan Council, and many other diocesan committees and boards. I am eager to thank all of them for what they have imparted to me. I want especially to thank the members of the Trustees' Investment Committee, which has been chaired over the years by William Herrman and Sherrill Blalock. Chapter 3 would have been impossible if I hadn't worked with them, though they are in no way responsible for any missteps in my discussion of investments.

I cannot acknowledge adequately how I have benefited from colleagues throughout the church. The parish administrators of our congregations large and small have taught us what we could do to support them in their work. Their ideas have found their way into the pages that follow. My colleagues in other dioceses and the staff of the Episcopal Church Center and the Church Pension Group have been sources of incalculable knowledge and expertise.

Most of all, I am grateful to the clergy and lay leaders of the congregations of the Episcopal Diocese of New York. At conferences and meetings, one-on-one and on Sunday mornings, their devotion to the church and their dedication to its work continually humble me. No matter how difficult the discussion, how late the meeting, or how far the drive afterward, I am always energized by having been with people who love the Lord Jesus and Christ's Body the Church. I cannot thank them sufficiently. The inspiration for almost everything in the pages that follow came either during one of those conversations, or in the car on the way home when it finally occurred to me what I might have said and how I might have said it.

Staten Island, New York
Feast of Hugh, Bishop of Lincoln
November 17, 2005

Introduction

This book is the outgrowth of my reflections on uncounted meetings and conversations I've had with the clergy and lay leaders of the congregations of the Episcopal Diocese of New York over the ten years I have served on the diocesan staff. Whatever there is of use in the pages that follow is the result of my observing the same dynamics in different congregations until I could not fail to notice certain common themes and patterns.

As with most patterns, once you've seen it here, you start to see it over here and over there as well. Although I am an Episcopalian living in the Northeast, I believe the attitudes and situations to which I call attention exist in congregations of other denominations or faiths, and, indeed, in many not-for-profit organizations. I hope that leaders of all congregations and other organizations find the discussion accessible.

I have not always been a New York Episcopalian. I was raised in the American Baptist Church in a small central Indiana town. We frequently visited my grandparents' Methodist church in an even smaller county seat in western Indiana. In addition, the life of the minuscule Baptist congregation my great-grandparents had helped found, close to the nearby family farm, was an ever-present topic of discussion. I prepared for ordination at Princeton Theological Seminary and Yale Divinity School, each of which draws its student body from different parts of the spectrum of mainline denominations. I am grateful for all these formative influences, and, while I settled into the Episcopal tradition almost thirty years ago, I am always aware that there are other rooms in the household of faith. I hope that you find that awareness in what follows.

The Context I've Observed

The context of my observations has shaped what I have seen, and the context I've been looking at is the Episcopal Diocese of New York. The diocese comprises three boroughs of New York City (Manhattan, Staten Island, and the Bronx) and seven counties north and west of the city. Although there were rural areas in the northern counties until very recently, at this point the diocese is urban, suburban, and exurban. There are several factors I'd like to call out.

First, though we have some parishes of great size and prominence, the congregations in our diocese are mostly of small to medium size. Of our approximately two hundred congregations, 80 percent report 150 or fewer people in attendance on an average Sunday.

Second, although total parish income has been more than keeping up with inflation, there's less money in the congregations than there might be. About 60 percent of our congregations report $150,000 or less in annual operating income. Almost all report some level of long-term investments, but only about 25 percent of our parishes report investments of more than $1 million. Another 25 percent report less than $100,000 in investments.

Third, our congregations are venerable. About 175 of the total were founded before 1900. The New York area was thickly settled early, and the nineteenth-century missionaries did their work with great zeal in what was then the country. Over half of our church buildings, parish houses, and rectories are more than 125 years old. Many of our congregations have developed the habit of balancing the budget by deferring maintenance.

Fourth, stewardship in the diocese as a whole is not exemplary. Although giving has more than kept up with inflation, there is, with some exceptions, little tradition of proportional giving in our diocese. In 2003, the last year for which we have full statistics at this writing, the average annual pledge in our diocese was just over $1,600. This number does not compare favorably with the national average for the Episcopal Church ($1,791 in 2003), or with the statistics in other areas of the country.

Finally, our congregations, like those of many of the mainline churches, have come through a long period of decline in membership, although not usually a decline in income. It appears that, in many cases and in the diocese overall, the decline has stopped. Average Sunday attendance is about the same as it was fifteen years ago. Not all parishes are growing, but over half report growth, while twenty years ago, almost every congregation in our diocese was in decline.

I mention the decline of the last forty years because it has deeply affected the psyches of those who lead our congregations. In many cases they've been "managing decline" for so long that they've forgotten to look to the future. They view present needs only through the lens of past glories. This is very different from looking at the challenges of the present as a way to build toward the future.

Parishes that are "holding on" will be more likely to overdraw endowments to plug budget deficits. They'll sell property and spend the proceeds on current needs. They'll rent out so much of their space that there's no place to hold a coffee hour. In such a climate, the giving of members in support of the parish will likely be stagnant or disappointing.

Moreover, the skills that allow a parish to survive are not the skills that will permit growth. This is not a "church growth" book, but it's worth pointing out some dynamics that will hinder, and others that will help, the kind of strategic, forward-looking approach I advocate.

Parishes in survival mode centralize power in the hands of a few. Because they're trying to maintain the past, it's difficult for them to welcome newcomers. New members have to pay their dues, so to speak, before they can be trusted. These mechanisms usually work in the sense that they enable a congregation to survive. Centralization means that a small group of people can do the work with little fuss and not very many meetings. And a few new people do manage to work their way into the parish, enabling it to continue to survive. The new people who stay usually adopt the mentality of survival; indeed, that's one of the reasons they were accepted into the group. You know you're visiting a parish in survival mode when the telephone message machine and the sign in front of the church tell you that there are services at 8:00 and 10:00 a.m., when there's really only one service at 9:00 a.m. If you find someone there at the time you come, you'll be told that "everybody knows" the time of the service. A parish can survive in this way for decades, particularly if the plant is not too big. The mechanisms of survival prevent growth, but they do enable survival.

By contrast, a growing parish tends to bring new people into activities quickly. A growing parish tries to disperse power so that lots of people feel they have a stake in the parish. A growing parish communicates broadly and repeatedly instead of relying on the grapevine and the expectation that "everybody knows" what is necessary. A growing parish grows because it offers something that stimulates and touches you right now, and it communicates a vital sense that there is a future here.

The primary assumption of this book is that the leaders of congregations need to believe that the congregation *has* a future if they are going to make appropriate decisions about how they manage the congregation's assets for the long term. In other words, if you don't think you have a future, you won't give much thought to the long-term implications of your decisions. It may seem too obvious to need stating, but the consequences of this attitude need to be drawn out and an alternative approach articulated. That's my purpose in the pages that follow.

Do you think your parish has a future? Or do you just hope the doors stay open long enough for you to be buried from the parish you love? I've not heard vestry members ask themselves this question very often. When I've raised it in meetings with parish leaders, there have been a few uncomfortable silences as some people realize, perhaps for the first time, that they have no confidence or hope for the future of their parish. On other occasions people have realized that, despite the problems about which they've just been complaining, they have an underlying confidence that God has a future in mind for their parish. Sometimes, with that realization, the discussion has been able to move in a more constructive direction.

In short, a great deal of my work has been with

- smallish congregations that

- don't have a great deal of money, but

- have significant plants to maintain, and

- have a record of stewardship less vital than one might hope, and

- have also suffered something of a crisis of confidence.

If one or more of those qualities applies to your congregation, I think you'll find something useful here. If, on the other hand, you are a member of a large, rich congregation that's always been growing and has never had a problem with buildings or personal stewardship... well, maybe this book is for just about everyone after all!

I hope that the most helpful thing about this book is its emphasis on assets — the land and buildings the parish owns and the money it controls. You may initially find my discussion of a congregation's membership as "current assets" off-putting, but I ask you please to read that section before you decide that I am trying to think of people as one might think of widgets. That's not the point at all.

Finances and Program Work Together

If my main assumption is that your congregation has a future that you need to take into account as you make decisions, my main goal is to bridge the gap that often exists between the theological, spiritual, or programmatic side of the parish and the financial side. Typically, clergy feel more comfortable speaking of the former but feel intimidated or impatient when it comes to finances. Laypeople typically feel inadequate with regard to theology but competent to speak about money.

The way people talk past each other on these matters can have serious long-term consequences. Enthusiastic and well-designed revitalization or church-growth efforts are often subverted, and the parish is permanently weakened by decisions to overspend what's left of the endowment or to dispose of property at below-market value. Or the effort never gets off the ground because those who control the purse strings lack any vision of what the money is meant to do.

Clergy and lay leaders need to have a basic familiarity with both kinds of language and concepts. Unlocking a future for a parish is like opening a safety deposit box: there are two keys that need to be turned simultaneously. For a congregation the keys are (1) a meaningful liturgical, pastoral, educational, and mission program suited to the parish and its community; and (2) the generation and management of assets to fund the program and keep it going over the long term. I want to concentrate on the second key, but I hope it is clear that the goal is not to increase our assets just to store them in bigger barns. The purpose of visionary financial leadership, prudent asset management, and good administration is to provide the resources necessary for the work of the church. In fact, it is usually not possible to generate resources unless (1) you have communicated a compelling vision of why you need the money, and (2) you have demonstrated the capacity to use your resources wisely and effectively.

Some Unique Aspects of Congregations

I'd like to lay out a bit more of the foundation on which this book rests. Churches are different from corporations or small businesses. I absolutely *do not* mean that churches don't need to reconcile their bank statements, maintain clear internal controls appropriate for their size, use good management practices, or have an annual independent audit. Good management is good management, whatever the enterprise.

However, some aspects of churches are different from those of businesses. Here are some differences that are relevant to the discussion in the chapters that follow.

1. *The proclamation of the gospel and the formation of Christian community are both unchanging and site-specific purposes.* Corporations and entrepreneurs do not need to stay in the same line of business; large corporations can diversify and change their core businesses completely, and, as we know, they can move lots of their operations around the globe. The church's mission does not change (though the way that mission is enacted and pursued may change), and a congregation has to assemble in some *place*. The church is global, but each worshiping congregation is and must be local. However well congregations use the Internet — and most could improve their use of it — I believe their fundamental dynamic will always be that people *congregate* to worship, to be converted by Word and Sacrament, and to be formed by opportunities for generosity, education, and service.

2. *Churches are perpetual institutions.* I do not mean that they *will* last forever, but they must *act as if* they will last forever. Both parts of the preceding are important. There is no magic to repeating, "the temple of the Lord, the temple of the Lord, the temple of the Lord," but there is usually no inherent reason that a congregation has to fail at any given point. Congregations are not bought out

or taken over. Unlike individuals, they do not have a natural life expectancy, although congregations certainly have died for all kinds of reasons. This point has tremendous implications that we explore in the chapters that follow. Churches and not-for-profits must be led and managed with an eye toward the most distant horizon conceivable. Every decision having to do with land, buildings, investments, and stewardship has long-term implications that the leadership must take into account.

3. *Churches are local membership organizations, and church leadership is immediately accountable to the membership.* This is another huge difference between churches and any for-profit organization. Stockholders often have little knowledge of the internal workings of the organization; the results that count are in the dividend and stock price. Privately held companies can be quite secretive. Transparency is a new corporate buzzword in the aftermath of recent scandals of corporate governance, but in healthy congregations the lay and ordained leaders have always acted with transparency because, as the saying goes, "The parish is a fishbowl." Unwise clergy and lay leaders have tried to act as if the parish were not, or should not be, a fishbowl, and they have often come to grief. Wise clergy and lay leaders have always made sure that the inner surface of the fishbowl is clean and the water is clear so that the congruence of their words and actions — both in their leadership roles and in their personal lives — is plainly visible to the membership. The leadership of a congregation must be accountable in ways that business leaders would find unnecessary, invasive, or even unlawful.

Another aspect of this immediate accountability is that the leadership must share the right amount of information in the right format with the congregation. We talk at various points in this book about accountability, because without accountability there can be no trust, and trust is essential to life in community. Too much unimportant, poorly organized financial information is in some ways more annoying and more destructive of trust than no information at all. At times I've been pretty sure that the treasurer or accountant *intended* to mystify the rest of the leadership and congregation by handing out pages of undigested and indigestible figures that didn't answer any basic questions.

Denomination-Neutral Vocabulary

Finally, I would like to say a word about terminology. In almost every denomination, the primary responsibility for leading the congregation and preserving the health of the congregation's assets rests with a group of local leaders, usually chaired by the ordained leader. Very often this group forms the corporation that owns, and holds in trust for the church, the real estate, the buildings, and the financial assets of the parish and of all its organizations. There are almost as many esoteric words for this group (e.g., vestry, session, classis, administrative board) as there are denominations. In addition, denominations all have some kind of regional and national judicatory structures, and there are even more words at these levels (diocese, synod, presbytery, convention, association, etc.).

My hope is that this book will be useful to the leaders of any congregation, and I endeavor not to undermine the utility of what follows through obstacles of mere terminology, so I ordinarily use language that is denomination-neutral. In general, "congregational leaders" means the vestry or local governing board, and "judicatory" means the regional authority (synod, diocese, presbytery, convention).

On the other hand, I value the smooth flow of language, and at times the neutral locution would impede understanding by making the sentence strange. In these cases, I use the terminology familiar to me, and you will occasionally encounter "rector," "vestry," and "diocese" referring respectively to the ordained leader, the lay and ordained congregational leaders, and the judicatory.

I've given you an idea of where I'd like to take you, and I've indicated something about the way I plan to go and the baggage I'm taking along.

André Gide said, "That education is best which runs counter to you." I've found that there's real value in studying points of view that are not mine. On the other hand, the most exciting things I've read are ones that put into words things I realize I've dimly thought or known. I hope this book both runs counter to you in a stimulating way and gives you some moments of recognition as well.

Chapter 1

Leadership for the Long Haul

For surely I know the plans I have for you, says the Lord, plans for your welfare and not for harm, to give you a future with hope. —Jeremiah 29:11

Many congregational leaders may feel that it is a big enough job to deal with the demands and the crises of the present moment. A boiler breakdown, the unexpected loss of a major pledge, getting the bills paid and the fair organized — if we deal with all of those things, isn't that enough?

Well, no, it's not enough. It's not enough just to react to whatever happens and keep the normal round of things going. Leaders also must *lead.* You may think you lack training to be a leader, but being a leader isn't primarily a matter of skills. Leadership is more an attitude than a technique. It's more of an approach to situations than a skill. For a congregation, leadership means things like the following:

- taking the long view
- having a vision on the horizon and working toward it
- causing something to happen that would not have happened in the normal course of events
- preparing to leave your successors an institution stronger than it was when you began to lead it

What these things have in common is a concern for the future. Leadership points toward the future. When there is a lack of leadership

23

it is always because those who run your congregation have forgotten (or don't believe) this crucial truth: *your congregation has a future.* When money is tight, and there don't seem to be enough people, and you can't keep up with the maintenance of the buildings, it's easy to forget this simple truth: *your congregation has a future.* When your congregation's past seems brighter and more prosperous than its present state, it easy to lose sight of this important truth: *your congregation has a future.*

Why do leaders forget about the future of the institutions they lead? Those most likely to forget are those who are consumed with anxiety about the problems of the present, and this is too bad, because decisions made in anxiety are likely to be shortsighted decisions. Shortsighted decisions make the situation worse, which in turn makes people more anxious. Anxiety is contagious, and it feeds on itself.

You can always tell when you're meeting with people who are used to being anxious. Two things happen during the meeting. First, the group spends the most time talking about the least important items. The discussion of the financial report may take forty-five minutes to an hour, but the discussion focuses on the least important numbers. Second, there are likely to be a fair number of complaints and negative comments.

Both of these dynamics are signs of anxious people looking for safety. It's much safer to talk about why the AA group is contributing only $12 a meeting this year instead of the $15 they gave last year than it is to talk about the decrease in the number of pledgers or the $30,000 budget deficit. It's also safer to be negative when everyone is anxious: when people are anxious and depressed, the negative voice is likely to be right that the fair won't raise as much money as the organizers dare to hope.

Anxiety is nearsighted. Anxiety focuses our attention on the concerns and the crises of the present moment, and we lose the long view. It's as if we were looking so closely at the ground where our feet are standing that we can no longer see where we are going. Indeed, we lose sight of the fact that we're going anywhere at all, so we just stop moving at all and let things move at us.

Anxiety is lonesome. Anxiety makes us feel that we are isolated, that no one else has a situation like ours, and that no one can help. The congregations that feel the most defeated, the least hopeful that anything can change or get better, are the ones that are the most strongly convinced that their problems are theirs alone, that no one else shares similar ones, and that no one cares about theirs. Of course every congregation is to some extent different from every other one — no two groups of people are exactly alike — but the little ways in which congregations differ are far less important than the ways they are alike.

Anxiety makes us vulnerable to negative dynamics, makes us forget that we have a future, and makes us feel that we're all alone. So the more space anxiety occupies in the organization, the less room there is for leadership.

Lack of leadership is a lack of faith in the future. But if we don't have it, how do we get that faith? Well, most of us started to attend church regularly *before* we had received the gift of faith in Christ. We received the gift of faith because we were already acting *as if* we believed. I think it's the same with the gift of faith in the future. There is only one way out of the debilitating anxiety that saps leaders' strength and shortens their vision. The only way out of anxiety is to lead. Begin acting *as if* you have a future, and God may very well give you one.

The foundation of leadership is remembering that the congregation has a future and that the congregation is not alone. If, in every deliberation, you remember that you have a future, your highest priority will be leaving to the next group of leaders a parish that is stronger than it was when you became a leader. If, in every deliberation, you remember that you are not alone, you will constantly call on the experiences of other clergy and congregations, the agencies in your community, and the resources of your judicatory and national organization.

Congregational leaders must certainly act to meet current needs, but they must always balance the needs of the present with the long-term interests and health of the congregation. Too often leaders take actions that seem expedient or pastoral or mission-minded at the time, but down the road it becomes sadly apparent to your successors that these decisions seriously compromised the long-term ability of the congregation to carry out its mission.

When leaders sell or lease property unwisely, or make the cheapest, rather than the most appropriate, building improvements, or pull too much out of their long-term investments for capital improvements or operating expenses, they are forgetting that they have a future.

Congregational leaders must think of the congregations they lead as perpetual institutions. "Perpetual" here does not mean that the congregation *will* last forever; it means that the leaders of the congregation must act *as if* it will last forever. In perpetual institutions, a short-term solution is no solution at all. The leaders of perpetual institutions must always take the long view, even when meeting current needs.

If the congregation's leaders cultivate the proper attitude of making the best decisions for the long-term health of the congregation, that attitude itself may also begin to clear away other common impediments to effective leadership.

For example, in congregations large and small, one person sometimes dominates the leadership group. All too often the dominant person — especially if he or she has been in power for many years — does not exercise good leadership, but uses the position either to work out a personal agenda or to control others. If the rest of the leadership takes the long view and constantly brings the conversation back to the merits of the case, there will be less chance of descending into a power struggle or a mere squabble.

My aim is to help leaders of congregations make decisions that are in the long-term best interests of their congregations. In order to make such decisions, the leaders need to believe that the congregation has a future, but that's not all they need. A few other things get in the way of leaders making good decisions about the assets their congregations have. When we consider that so much property has been sold, so many long-term investments dissipated, and so many buildings allowed to deteriorate, we must ask why we have made such shortsighted decisions so often. I think there are several reasons that so many congregations and judicatories have done a less than exemplary job of good asset management over the years. These are different ways of forgetting either the future or the context in which we're operating.

The Difficulty and Expense of Managing Assets

It isn't easy to own something and to take care of it. Nothing — not property, nor buildings, nor investments, nor a congregation — takes care of itself. The resources needed to manage property or an investment portfolio generally don't exist in-house. A well-led and well-managed institution like a hospital or college would find appropriate arms-length professional assistance to help with property or investment management, but congregations opt again and again either (1) to do without proper guidance in the management of their assets, or (2) to put themselves at the mercy of someone who agrees to do it for free, or (3) to allow themselves to be vastly overcharged by someone personally connected to a leader.

After a time of unsatisfactory results and constant headaches, the leaders decide they would be better off if they disposed of the asset. If it's a piece of property, the leaders are often so frustrated that they agree to sell the property for less than market value, just to get the problem off the agenda every month. If it's money, the decision to dispose of the asset may be less explicit. When meeting with a vestry that's overspending its endowment, I've sometimes had the impression that they're almost *trying* to spend it down so they won't have to deal with the responsibility of getting proper management for the investments.

If you don't want to be a slave to what you own, you need to pay attention to your assets, think long-term about them, and get the appropriate assistance you need to take care of them. We're stewards of the gifts and talents God has entrusted to us in our generation. Not only, as I truly believe, will we be called to give an account of our stewardship to God, but, believe me, our successors will be able to tell whether or not we've done a good job. For good or ill, they'll live with the long-term consequences of our decisions.

Note to the clergy

The "professional staff" of a congregation often consists of only you. You probably didn't come to ordination with either a background or a huge interest in finance and property management. And even though you have to spend a great deal of your time on these matters, you may remember that, in seminary, you received the explicit or implicit message that this isn't your job. Seminaries pay little, if any, attention to these matters. I think this is very unfortunate. It may not be the job of seminaries to *teach* these things (on the other hand, perhaps it *is* part of the job of a professional school to prepare students for the profession), but this area of congregational life is definitely part of your responsibilities. You may have expected that others would deal with these things. Your lay leaders probably expected that you would. Since resentment stems from disappointed expectations, there may now be some resentment all around. No matter how hard volunteers work or how much time they have available, the "executive director" is going to have a major role in these matters — especially when you are probably the facilities manager and perhaps part of the janitorial staff as well. My very sympathetic advice is: don't kick against the goad. Try considering that financial leadership and the good management of the institution's assets are opportunities for ministry (they really are). Learn to be comfortable with the basic categories, get the outside help you need, and do a good job with it. Your ministry will be more effective, and your successor will thank you very much.

The Tyranny of the Present and the Local

We're born and educated and formed in particular places at a particular moment in history. Those places and that moment have their own experiences, convictions, assumptions, and prejudices. These things fill our minds so that we're not usually consciously aware of them. They're just part of the way things are. Just remember this: things change over time. The things people took for granted a century ago are different from what we assume is "normal." We may safely predict that future generations will not make the same assumptions we do.

So we are probably not the culmination of history. We are probably not the point to which the trajectory of the cosmos has been tending; we are more likely part of the trajectory. In other words, we must see our needs and our priorities in the context of the priorities and needs of the past and those of the future. It's self-centered — but not uncommon — to imagine that the present crisis (there's always at least one) is more important than anything that's likely to follow, so we should spend all we have on meeting today's needs. Sometimes this is the pathology of an egocentric (but usually charismatic) leader. In other cases this is an error into which earnest people who are concerned for others are prone to fall, but it is an error nevertheless. It's a way of forgetting the future.

Related to this is the economist Herbert Stein's memorable observation, "Unsustainable trends tend not to be sustained." An examination of any past trend — think of the Dow Jones average that, it was said through the late 1990s, couldn't go down — demonstrates the truth of Stein's words. However, it's very difficult for us to apply the words to any trend that we are currently experiencing because such a trend is part of the way things are. We may not even be aware of it as something that *could* change. As a boy in 1962, I heard a presentation on the unbelievable number of schools that would need to be constructed assuming, as everyone did, that the high birthrate that began in 1946 would simply continue. Of course, 1962 was about the time the birthrate began to fall.

When somebody says, "assuming that present trends continue," allow yourself to spend at least a moment thinking, "Yeah, but what if they don't?" Resist the tyranny of the present and the local. It'll make you a bit of a contrarian, so be careful, but it's a very useful corrective to whatever the received consensus of the group is at the moment. You'll make better decisions for the future if you hang a little loose to the present and its apparently unchangeable trends.

The Thought That "Church Is Different"

A lot of congregational leaders and clergy know that the church is different from other institutions in society, but they may be less clear on where and how the church is different and whether there are any models that can help. Clergy and church people often think they should be suspicious of other models: how spiritual or theologically sound can secular models be? Because of this not always well-articulated sense that "church is different," leaders can make unsound decisions that lack even basic common sense and tell themselves that they are decisions of faith and that God will provide.

I have already said that I think the business model is not where we ought to look, but there are some helpful models for church leadership and management.

We shouldn't look to the private sector. Businesses don't have endowments, for one thing, and there's no concept of a perpetual institution in the for-profit world. If there are useful models for us, they exist in the enormous not-for-profit sector that's grown up in the last half-century. It makes sense that not-for-profits have something to say to us because a huge number of not-for-profit institutions — schools, colleges and universities, museums and other cultural organizations, hospitals and agencies that provide social and community services — were originally church institutions or were begun by committed church people to meet some need. A church certainly differs in organizational dynamics because of the unique immediacy of a congregation's membership — no college has an open meeting for all students and alumni every week! — but universities manage their investments for the long term and usually have old, historic buildings to take care of. And they're not doing all that *instead of* concentrating on their primary mission; they're doing it *so that* they can do a better job fulfilling their primary mission.

Of course, there are differences of scale. Only the very largest congregations have as many professional and support staff as the smallest college. Funding patterns are very different. The entire secular not-for-profit sector has grown because of government funding — subsidies for cultural institutions, contracts for services for social service agencies, and tuition grants and guaranteed loans for undergraduate and graduate students. However, congregations can learn much from the not-for-profit model, because not-for-profits are also perpetual institutions with investments, buildings, and a constituency. Many parts of the not-for-profit sector roll smoothly on the wheels congregational leaders spend hours in isolation trying to invent.

The Future: Something You're Moving Toward, or Something Coming at You?

There are two ways to conceive of the future, and which of the two dominates our thinking makes a significant difference in how we lead. We can think of the future as something *we're moving toward,* or we can think of the future as *something moving toward us.*

If we think of the future as something we are moving toward, then we will be actively involved in creating the future. Planning, prediction, and preparation will be paramount. If we are moving toward the future, then the future will be something we make, or, at least, the future will be something over which our efforts have a great influence.

If, on the other hand, we think of the future as something that is moving toward us, then there will be a certain passivity in our approach. There will be an emphasis on the unexpected and on the things that are beyond our control. *Que será será* is an expression that can be facetious, resigned, or ominous.

It is not all one or the other. The future is not an event; the future is a Person. If we're moving toward the future, we're not studying for an exam: we're working to build a better, closer relationship with the God revealed in Jesus Christ our Lord. If the future is moving toward us, we don't need to fear: it is God coming to meet us.

God is our future. Because he loves us so much, he is moving toward us every moment, calling out our name: "beloved," "not forsaken." God is the future that is coming at us.

God is our future. Because we love him and want to be like him and want to be with him, we are moving toward him every moment. God is the future we long for and toward which we are moving.

Because we have this confidence that God is moving toward us and we are moving toward God, we can do our part in leading our congregations into the future God is preparing for us.

Chapter 2

Straight Talk about Your Assets

O merciful Creator, your hand is open wide to satisfy the needs of every living creature: Make us always thankful for your loving providence; and grant that we, remembering the account that we must one day give, may be faithful stewards of your good gifts....
— Book of Common Prayer, page 259

Most congregations own property and buildings and have some money in the bank and some level of investments. God has not given us these resources as ends in themselves. The purpose of any congregation's real property and financial assets is to support the work of its people in proclaiming the gospel, forming Christians and ministering Christ's reconciling justice and love in the community. Congregational leaders must remember the future so the assets they manage can continue to support the ministry of the congregation over the long term.

There are four kinds of assets. They are not interchangeable. Each requires a different kind of strategic management to achieve its purpose over the years. As we'll see, however, all four kinds of assets are interrelated and work together in their own way so that your congregation is strengthened to do its work. The four kinds of assets are (1) **land**, (2) **long-term investments**, (3) **buildings**, and (4) **current assets:** (*a*) the commitment and support of your current congregation, and (*b*) the reserve funds you have that are available to spend for various purposes.

This chapter presents an overview of the different kinds of assets. I discuss investments, buildings, and the support of your current congregation in much more detail in the chapters that follow. Although we start with permanent assets and end with current assets, all of your assets are important. I discuss the financial commitment of your congregation last because there's the most to say about that topic.

Let me offer a word to challenge as well as encourage you. First, the challenge. As we will see, assets do not manage themselves. Everything you are responsible for as a leader of your congregation requires thoughtful strategic management. Buildings don't take care of themselves. There is no risk-free way to manage investments. Your decisions and your leadership affect your congregation's morale and commitment for good or for ill. God has put all these things into our care for a time, and our stewardship of them matters; our decisions have consequences that are no less real because it may take some years for them to become visible.

Now the encouragement. You do not have to be an expert to be a leader. You don't need to be an investment broker or a property manager to make good decisions about these matters. You do need to be willing to seek out expert advice and counsel when it is appropriate, and, though this may seem anathema for good, stingy church people, you have to be willing to *pay* for appropriate and necessary professional services. Don't jump at quick fixes. Try to analyze whatever you are discussing from the vantage point of thirty or forty years from now. When your grandchildren, or other people's grandchildren, are sitting around this table, how will the decision you're making now appear to them then? You *can* be a good and faithful steward simply by holding in mind the long-term implications of your decisions and getting the professional counsel you need.

Land — One of Two Things That Should Last

Many congregations tend to think of the land and the buildings together; that's why they often have Buildings and Grounds committees. Your land, however, unlike your buildings, is a perpetual asset. Unless you're on the oceanfront, you can pretty much count on your land not to grow or shrink. Your land tends to increase in value over time, if only because, as they say, God's not making any more of it.

It is risky, however, to convert the value of land into money. Congregations — and judicatories — have sold a great deal of property over the years, and subsequent generations have often been short-changed as a result. The principal risk is this: land is an illiquid asset that can't be spent. Once you have turned land into a liquid asset — money — it's all too easy for it to disappear. It can dry up if it is not invested to maintain its value with respect to inflation; it can leak away over a period of years if you overdraw it; or it can be spilled out in a torrent of ill-considered spending.

There are several drawbacks to selling property, obvious in hindsight, but often overlooked at the time. First, when we sell property, we receive only its value at a particular moment in time. We lose the future appreciation. (And that assumes that the property was sold for its current market value; too often it is not.) Second, when we sell property, it's gone, and it is usually impossible to recover and too expensive to replace.

There is often a third drawback. Owning an improved property and using it for your purposes is usually cheaper than generating the resources you need to buy the equivalent each year. For example, if you sell the rectory and invest the proceeds so you can pay the cleric a cash housing allowance, the drawdown you can prudently take from the amount invested will probably be significantly less than the amount of the cash housing allowance you need to come up with every year. Let's say that you sell a rectory, parsonage, or manse of ample size for $350,000, and you invest the proceeds in accordance with the guidelines we discuss later in the section on investments. You will prudently be able to draw 4 percent to 5 percent per year from the fund. That works out to between $14,000 and $17,500 annually. Given the cost of renting or purchasing a house in many parts of the country, and given the minimum clergy compensation guidelines most denominations or regional judicatories have, you will probably have to pay the clergyperson a cash housing allowance greater than the amount you can prudently draw from the proceeds you've invested from the sale of the house.

There is yet another downside to selling the clergy housing in many parts of the country. In the northern area of our diocese, housing prices were fairly reasonable a generation ago. If the parish sold the house and paid the clergy a cash housing allowance, the clergy could get equity in the housing market, and the parish wouldn't have the headache of maintaining the house. For a time, perhaps, everyone was a winner. Housing prices in our area have now risen so dramatically that parishes find it difficult to call clergy from other parts of the country where housing prices are lower. Most clergy can't buy into the market, and the parishes can't pay enough to make up the difference between what the cleric can sell the old house for and what it takes to buy something comparable. Though I know some would disagree on this point, I suggest that, in expensive housing markets at least, the old model of church-provided housing might be best after all. Some financial planners think it is better to save for retirement through tax-deferred savings than through the housing market. If you still have a rectory, parsonage, or manse, think very long and very hard before you sell it or convert it to Sunday school rooms and office space. If it is best for the current cleric not to live there, keep it and rent it out; it may be best for your next cleric to live in the house.

The amount of property owned today by all Episcopal institutions in the Diocese of New York is a fraction of the property they have owned in the past. Several early parishes owned glebes (farmland that supported the priest) or had other land holdings. Few of these landed endowments remain, and in no case I'm aware of did the congregation preserve the proceeds of the sale. We are collectively less able to make Christ known and to minister effectively because we have spent part of the patrimony that could have funded our mission over the long term.

Here are some recent painful examples from my part of the vineyard. In the midst of the fiscal crisis of the 1970s, when many despaired of the future of New York City and its institutions, it seemed to be a good idea to let a community-based not-for-profit take title to the venerable but derelict Church of the Holy Communion on Sixth Avenue at Twentieth Street. However, since no restriction as to use was put in the deed, the 1840s landmark structure designed by Richard Upjohn soon became more notorious as a drug-infested disco and club than it had been previously celebrated for the legacy of its innovative founding rector, William A. Muhlenburg. In upstate villages, we have donated to the local government church buildings rendered superfluous by a merger. The merged parish, of course, would rather have received some endowment funds from a market-rate sale. Both parishes and the diocesan corporation have sold rectories and vicarages in places where clergy housing is now a problem. An urban parish recently has been forced to sell a building lot it had held for thirty years in order to pay current bills.

If you examine the history of your own congregation or denomination, you may find a similar pattern. If you do find such a pattern, there's nothing to do about it but to resolve from now on not to make decisions that your successors will find shortsighted. If you are fortunate enough not to find such a pattern, then thank God for the wisdom of your forebears, and resolve to emulate the good example they have left for your generation.

In most denominations, congregations are separately established and own their own assets. Sometimes, though, a congregation may need to acquire the approval of a denominational body for certain property transactions. In the Episcopal Church, parishes must have the approval of the bishop and a diocesan body of elected clergy and laity called the standing committee to sell property, to take out a mortgage using property it owns as collateral, or to enter into a long-term lease of its property. I suggest that we should value, not resent, such checks and balances where they exist. If congregations must seek such permissions, I hope the approvals are not granted as a *pro forma* rubber-stamping of the congregation's decision. A review by a third party that has the long-term health of the congregation at heart provides a valuable opportunity to examine the proposed terms of the transaction. Whether or not you need anyone's permission, please make sure that any property transaction you contemplate is part of a long-term strategy for your congregation, not a quick fix to some current problem.

Land is a perpetual asset, but only if we keep the land or its value — adjusted at least for inflation — inviolate. If we sell it below its value or spend the proceeds from the sale, we have simply impoverished ourselves and our successors and made the church less able to carry on its work in the generations to come.

Long-Term Investments — The Other Perpetual Asset

Properly invested and prudently used, a congregation's long-term investments, or endowments, are the second perpetual asset. As with land, congregations usually own their own financial assets. The limitations that may be present on real estate transactions usually do not exist with regard to your investments. In other words, even if you need ecclesiastical or civil approvals to sell your property, you can probably overspend, or even deplete, your unrestricted investments without asking anyone's permission. Therefore, it is all the more important for you to exercise fiduciary responsibility and farsighted leadership with regard to your endowments. The constituency to whom you are accountable for your management of the investments isn't born yet. For example, your whole congregation may prefer to spend half your endowment to renovate the parish house rather than raise the resources necessary to do it from the current membership. What will those in the congregation thirty years from now think when it's time to do the parish house again and the money's gone?

Strictly speaking, an endowment is a gift restricted by the donor in such a way that the principal can never be spent, but what the original gift earns in income, and usually appreciation, can be used. An unrestricted gift that the congregation decides to invest and treat as an endowment is sometimes called a quasi-endowment. When most people speak of their endowments, they usually mean both true endowments and quasi-endowments. To avoid confusion, I use the phrase "long-term investments" to mean any funds, whether restricted by the donor or unrestricted, that your congregation has decided to treat as part of a long-term investment portfolio.

Here I must draw a crucial distinction. Long-term investments do *not* include the reserve funds that you're planning to spend or need to have available to spend. You *must* separate long-term investments from reserve funds; you cannot invest them in the same vehicles. We discuss this in greater detail later.

It might be a good idea here to point out how long-term investments and reserve funds in not-for-profits differ from the idea of working capital in businesses. I've known very successful business executives and investors who convince themselves that it is all right to use long-term investments for capital improvements because they see long-term investments as "working capital." In business, money is generally not held for its own sake. Money is meant to be spent on a warehouse, say, and trucks, so the business can make more money from the goods it hauls and resells. If it's a publicly traded corporation, in general, cash should be invested in the business or paid out in dividends to stockholders. It might seem to congregational leaders that spending several million dollars on upgrading the facilities is an investment of working capital that will pay off down the road. Please don't take that approach unless you really do have a plan for how to replace those long-term invested funds. Sure, you'll be more comfortable in a well-lighted and air-conditioned church, but how, exactly, is that going to pay off? More seriously, you were using the drawdown from that "working capital" to support the operating budget. Now you have a budget shortfall and depleted long-term investments, so you have a double whammy to make up. Long-term investments are not working capital. Whether donor-restricted or not, your long-term investments should be treated as endowments and kept inviolate.

The goals in managing long-term investments are simple:

1. You want to make sure that the growth of the funds keeps up with inflation so the investments maintain their purchasing power in constant dollars; and

2. You want a reasonably steady stream of money from the investments available every year to fund current needs, such as your capital reserve fund, the operating budget, or other programs.

Failure to accomplish *both of these goals simultaneously* means that the long-term investments will fall short of their purpose, which is to provide a stream of resources in constant dollars to help fund your mission in perpetuity. However, many congregations sabotage their futures by withdrawing too much from their investments or by not allowing the value to keep up with inflation. In fact, congregations can mismanage investments in all kinds of ways. Unfortunately, an excess of caution can be as bad in the long term as playing the market. The two most common ways to mismanage investments are (1) taking out too much, and (2) ignoring the effects of inflation.

On the one hand, too many congregations simply draw from their investments whatever it takes to plug a budget deficit, which can be disastrous. If, over the long term, you draw out more than the funds have earned after taking inflation into account, the value of the investments will be reduced or depleted. Your successors in office will not thank you for your poor stewardship.

On the other hand, some think they are playing it safe if the funds are all (or nearly all) invested in fixed-income instruments like bonds, and they pull down all the interest. This approach appears to be risk-free. You have little or no exposure to the risks of an unpredictable stock market, and you're taking out no more than the income you earn. However, over the long term, this strategy fails to achieve either of your investment goals. Because there's little or no capital growth with fixed-income investments, inflation erodes the purchasing power of the principal, and your income stream in real dollars diminishes every year. The effects of inflation may seem small from year to year, but they become obvious over a few decades. For example, in 1960, the $6,000 you could earn in interest on $150,000 invested in bonds at 4 percent was sufficient in many parts of the country to fund many a cleric's salary and benefits. What percentage of that package can $6,000 pay today?

There is no way to remove risk from investment management. There is both the risk of the stock market and the risk of inflation. Chapter 3 discusses the best practices of managing the risks of having long-term investments. Remember, the aim is both to protect the investments' purchasing power and to make funds available every year to support your work.

Buildings — The Asset That Requires Resources

The buildings congregations own are certainly assets. In many cities and towns, the public buildings of greatest beauty are church buildings. Regardless of architectural merit, church buildings are where people have met God and celebrated the pivotal events of their lives. There are parish houses that are hubs of community activity, and there are houses that have sheltered generations of clergy and their families. These are all great assets, and we want them to last, both for their beauty and for their utility.

But buildings are *depreciable* assets. That is, they require a steady stream of funds to keep them in good repair as their various systems and components wear out. And, unlike a typical family that owns a house for a period of years and then sells it, a perpetual institution can never expect to recover the funds used in the repairs. Homeowners planning to sell their houses at retirement may take money from savings in order to renovate the kitchen, knowing that the improvement increases the resale value. In other words, they'll get the benefit of using a renovated kitchen for several years, and then they'll recoup a good part of the money they spent on the kitchen because they'll be able to sell for a higher price. Since congregations do not typically sell their plants and move elsewhere — and if you did, who'd buy them? — you must simply be prepared every twenty years or so to furnish the resources necessary to renovate the parish house kitchen — and for goodness' sake, don't forget the one in the rectory!

If you take the long view — the only view congregational leaders can responsibly take — drawing extra funds from the long-term investments to make capital improvements is not a good idea, because the effect of this is to convert what should be a perpetual asset (the long-term investments) into a depreciable asset (the buildings). And yet this disadvantageous dissipation of assets occurs regularly in churches. Some congregations sold their parsonages and used a major part of the proceeds to refurbish the parish house. That transaction may have seemed like a good idea at the time, but a generation later the rectory is gone, no funds remain from its sale, and it's time to fix up the parish house again.

It is also important to ensure that the buildings do not deteriorate through deferred maintenance. Deferring maintenance is like buying your groceries on a credit card and making only the minimum payment every month. It creates a debt you or your successors will have to pay with ruinous interest. The "interest rate" on deferred maintenance is high because almost every building maintenance issue starts out small, growing geometrically at first, then exponentially. If you don't prevent a problem or get it when it starts, somebody will end up paying a lot more later on. As we will see in chapter 4, foresight, regular attention, and some astonishingly simple habits can prevent many problems or stop them while they're small. The simplest thing to do is to inspect the buildings inside and out several times a year. I don't mean you need to hire a professional; I mean just walk around and look. See if the leaders are connected to the gutters. See if the leaders are carrying the water far enough away from the foundation. Are there shingles missing? Is there anything inside that indicates water intrusion? Make a note of the little things that need taking care of, and then *take care of them.*

Every congregation that owns a building needs to figure out a way to put money every year into a capital reserve account to fund regular capital maintenance. The easiest way to do this is to identify a regular source of income to devote to this purpose. That income stream could be all or part of the amount you take from your investments; it could be the proceeds of an annual fund-raising event, or it could be a line in your budget. Whatever the source of the funds, and especially if it is a budget line, the amount should be *transferred* to a short-term reserve account earning interest. Money market accounts, CDs, or even passbook savings accounts are the appropriate place for reserve funds. If you are not setting aside money every year into a capital reserve account, you are almost certainly deferring maintenance. Chapter 4 addresses these matters at more length.

Buildings — The Asset That Provides Resources

Buildings require maintenance, but buildings are also potential sources of revenue as well as opportunities for mission. Almost all congregations regularly make their space available to groups for meetings, but many congregations also rent out part of their space both to provide a community service and to generate revenue.

It is not necessarily a sign of decline that congregations have spaces they no longer need for their own programs. It is a sign of changing times. Between roughly 1870 and 1930, many congregations built "institutional" parish houses with auditoriums, gymnasiums, and even bowling alleys. In those years, our congregations were for young people centers of activities that the public schools and other organizations now provide. Church buildings can still be used intensively for programs that serve the community, but the financial arrangements will be different. For example, an organization with outside funding might provide the services, and the congregation will lease its spaces to the program.

The arrangements between the congregation and the outside groups that use the congregation's space are often vague and messy, however. The purpose of good leases and space use agreements is not to be petty and bureaucratic; rather, the purpose of such agreements is to set up the structure in which a mutually beneficial relationship can thrive. You must know whether the income you receive for the use of the space is reasonable; there must be careful discussions about schedules and storage when arrangements are made; and there must be structures in place to keep lines of communication open and to deal with problems as they arise. Chapter 5 goes into more detail about arrangements with outside groups.

People Are Your Primary Current Asset

Current assets are the resources you have available to you right now to serve the congregation's mission. Strictly in money terms, that means (1) your current income from contributions, rent, fund-raisers, and the drawdown available from your investments, and (2) surplus operating funds from previous years and the money you've set aside in various reserve funds for particular purposes.

Since your current income comes mostly from the gifts and efforts of the membership, the commitment and support of the current members of your congregation are your principal current assets. Your current members are the part of the communion of saints available on earth now to do the work God is giving us to do. No other kind of asset can substitute for a vital, committed assembly of formed Christians who are ready both in mind and body to "accomplish with free hearts those things which belong to [God's] purpose" (BCP, p. 229).

Such people "work, pray, and give for the spread of the kingdom of God" (BCP, p. 856). In this discussion, we focus on money, but I am mindful that leaders need to give the congregation the opportunity to do more than make financial gifts. The "pure offering" that Malachi 1:11 tells us God desires is not the bread, wine, and money that we bring to the altar. Those are signs of the real offering of "our selves, our souls and bodies" (BCP, p. 336). Without that real self-offering, the signs are empty. Money is an indispensable sign of our self-offering, but more than money is involved in that self-offering that God wants from us and that we want to give to God.

People support the church financially in three ways: (1) gifts to the current budget (annual giving), (2) gifts to special campaigns to raise endowment funds or make major improvements to the buildings (capital giving), and (3) gifts that often occur after death (planned giving).

To anyone who thinks it is inappropriate to speak of Christian formation as managing assets, I would say that my point is not to turn people into objects, valued only for their financial support. My point is to get leaders to understand fully that everything about a congregation requires good leadership and good management. The physical and financial assets congregations have are gifts that God has entrusted to our care for a time. The people in the congregation are also a gift, a gift that requires thoughtful, skillful handling. Parishes don't lead themselves, and no asset is self-managing. Perhaps because parish leaders have usually put their energy into dealing only with the things we usually think of as assets — property, investments, buildings — leaders may have been taking their primary current asset for granted. As a church leader, you might benefit from thinking about how to lead and how to manage your primary asset — the current congregation.

If the annual pledge campaign is disappointing, maybe it's not that the congregation's members are uncommitted or stingy. Maybe you've just assumed that they know what you know, and you haven't given them the information they need to understand the parish's finances. Or maybe the leadership doesn't practice and model good stewardship. You can't expect others to do what you're not doing.

Less-than-overwhelming enthusiasm for a capital campaign can result from many things. One might be that the congregation has watched the buildings deteriorate while funds have gone to other things, and they feel a little sullen about being asked to give more to take care of things that the leadership should have seen to along the way. Another might be a failure on the part of the leadership to "make the case" to the congregation that the parish needs the projects being proposed.

If nobody's left your congregation a bequest in recent years, it may not be a reflection of your members' faithlessness. It could be that you haven't asked regularly, as the rubric on page 445 of the Episcopal Prayer Book directs:

> *The Minister of the Congregation is directed to instruct the people, from time to time, about the duty of Christian parents to make prudent provision for the well-being of their families, and of all persons to make wills, while they are in health, arranging for the disposal of their temporal goods, not neglecting, if they are able, to leave bequests for religious and charitable uses.*

Or it could be that people are aware that the leadership has simply spent other bequests to plug budget deficits, and they don't want their "final gift" treated so cavalierly. It could be that other organizations asking for planned gifts (universities, community service organizations, or public television, for example) are doing a better job of outlining a vision for their futures that the gift would help to bring about.

If church leaders think of their congregation as one of the assets given into their care, they might begin to think in new ways and not take the people in the pews for granted. In chapter 6 we discuss how to provide responsible financial leadership of the people in your congregation and responsible fiscal management of the gifts they provide.

Finally, Your Reserve Funds

The other kind of asset congregations have are reserve funds — the money on deposit in the bank or invested short-term in money market accounts or CDs. Reserve funds include (1) surplus operating funds for immediate cash-flow needs and (2) funds you are accumulating that you know you will spend, as, for example, when the church raises money over a defined period to fix the roof. You know you will spend in the near term what you are raising.

There are two points to stress about reserve funds. First, they are crucial. If you are not setting aside funds from some source as a reserve for future needs, especially building needs, you are almost certainly deferring maintenance. If you are not reserving every year from some income stream an adequate amount for capital needs, it means that you have a deficit budget. Although the deficit might not appear on the financial reports presented to the annual meeting, the deficit becomes apparent over time in the gradual (and accelerating) deterioration of the buildings. It also means that you are funding your deficit by borrowing from the future. You can't provide leadership for the long term and prepare for your successors if you're funding a current deficit by mortgaging your future.

Second, reserve funds should *never* be invested in stocks or equities. This is why the first step in dealing with your money is to separate long-term investments from short-term reserves. Your long-term investments need to include investments in the stock market in order to benefit from the returns of equities that will come over the long haul. You can ride out the market cycles with your long-term investments because you are investing with the longest possible horizon. It is equally as vital that your reserve funds not be in stocks, because the market could be down at the point when you need to spend the funds.

Operating reserves and other reserve funds should be kept in money market funds and other interest-bearing accounts so that there is no short-term risk to the principal.

How It All Works Together

This overview shows how different kinds of assets require different kinds of strategic management, and explains how the different kinds of assets are interrelated and work together so you can do the work God is giving you to do.

A simple example shows how this approach works for the long-term good of the congregation. Imagine that you've sold the property a parishioner bequeathed you as a result of your planned-giving effort. The proceeds are now prudently invested, and the drawdown from the fund is transferred every quarter to your capital reserve fund. In other words, through a planned gift, a committed parishioner gave you land, one kind of permanent asset, which you've converted into long-term investments, the other permanent asset. The annual drawdown is paid into a reserve fund, a current asset, so that you can perform regular maintenance on your buildings, a depreciable asset.

Or perhaps in a similar instance, a member bequeathed the parish a house, and you decided to keep it and use it as a rental property. For a small percentage of the rent, a local property management firm finds and vets the tenants and collects the rent. The management company also deals with tenant complaints. (You don't want volunteers dealing with the most difficult parts of residential real estate rentals — "tenants and toilets.") You're putting part of the rent in a capital reserve fund to keep the house in rentable condition, and you're building up a vacancy reserve in case there is a period between tenants when there's no rent. The remainder of the rent helps fund a new after-school tutoring program.

In each case, a combination of farsighted leadership and careful management has strengthened the congregation's ability to fulfill its mission. Without an emphasis on planned giving, it might not have occurred to the parishioner to leave you the house. Without the discipline to manage well what you have, it would have been easy either to spend the proceeds of the sale on a renovation of the parish house, or to fail to reserve part of the rent to keep the house in good condition. By thinking things through and remembering the future, you will pass on to your successors a more vital parish in better shape to do the work God will call them to do.

In the chapters that follow, we take a closer look at investments, buildings, and the commitment of your current congregation. The pages that follow expand on this discussion, but by this time I hope I've communicated the substance of the book. If your congregation has a future, and if you are in a leadership role, then you need to think and act like a leader of an organization with a future. Becoming such a leader is not a matter of learning a list of skills or techniques in a workshop. It's catching a vision and being formed in what may be a new way of looking at your congregation and its life.

I hope that at least some who read this book will act differently in church board meetings from now on. If you've been depressed about the future of your congregation, I want you to feel more hopeful. If you've been feeling intimidated by these matters, I want you to be equipped so you feel more confident. If you've been a negative voice in meetings ("We can't do that"), I want you to be more positive ("What part of this could we get started on?"). If you've been controlling or domineering as a leader, I'd like you to understand that church leadership isn't about you; it's about God and the work God wants to do through the church. If you've been impatient with money discussions because you think it's in conflict with the mission of the church, I'd like you to see how farsighted management of what you have can result in more resources so that you can do more. This book is my contribution toward constructive, productive meetings of church boards that don't last more than ninety minutes.

I want more than good meetings, though. I'm after nothing less than a conversion experience. In the pages that follow and on the Web site that accompanies this book (*www.churchpublishing.org/rememberthefuture*), you will find lists, tips, guidelines, rules of thumb, and sample reports intended to be useful to you, but if you don't have a sense that your congregation has a future, they may seem disjointed or fussy. However, if you see yourself as a leader with a vision of the future of your congregation, and if you see how the decisions you make about your congregation's assets either implement or undermine that vision, then the things that follow will make sense as part of an ordered way of moving into the future that God, with your cooperation, is giving your congregation.

Chapter 3

Investments:
The Other Permanent Asset

And the one with two talents also came forward, saying, "Master, you handed over to me two talents; see, I have made two more talents." His master said to him, "Well done..."

— Matthew 25:22–23a

- Should we have endowments? Won't they hurt stewardship?

- How should our money be invested? Aren't CDs safer than stocks? Shouldn't we put the money in something that gives a return we can count on?

- Who should manage the investments? I like the guy who manages my retirement portfolio. Why don't we use him?

- How much should we use from the investments?

- What should we use money from the investments for?

- How can we tell from the statements how the investments are really performing?

- We're facing a building expense we didn't expect. Can't we take it from the endowment?

When it comes to endowments and investments, there are lots of questions. Many congregational leaders are unsure in this area. Some are dissatisfied with their current arrangements. Others ought to be.

54

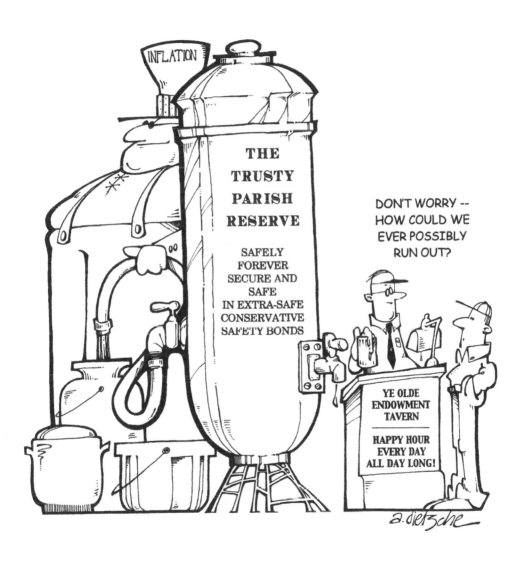

What Is an Endowment, and Should We Have One?

Strictly speaking, an "endowment" is a gift restricted by the donor in such a way that the principal can never be spent, but what the principal earns can be used. An unrestricted gift that the governing board decides to invest and treat as an endowment is sometimes called a "quasi-endowment." When most people say "endowments," they mean both "real" endowments and quasi-endowments. Here we use "long-term investments" to mean both. This term not only avoids confusion, but also makes it clear that the purpose of this money is to help further the congregation's mission over the long term.

Properly handled, long-term investments can be a useful and reliable source of funds for maintaining the buildings, helping the operating budget, or funding outreach programs. There are two distinct things about long-term investments that have to be handled properly.

First, of course, there's the money itself. It has to be allocated to different kinds of investments. It has to be managed so it maintains its purchasing power. It has to be tracked and reported on. It can't be overused, or it won't last. It has to be added to. This chapter is mostly concerned with suggestions for the proper handling of the money.

Second, the implications of long-term investments for steward-ship and individual giving must be handled properly. In the churches where I grew up there was a strong feeling that each generation was responsible for supporting the church from pledges and gifts the current membership made every year. People disapproved of en-dowments because they believed endowments would render good personal stewardship unnecessary. I strongly agree that trying to use "other people's money" to pay for the church is a constant temp-tation to church people — particularly when leaders don't model proportional giving and tithing. Other people's money is a theme to which we return, especially in chapter 6 when we discuss giving by the present congregation. However, the mere existence of long-term investments doesn't kill stewardship. Leaders kill, or fail to inspire, stewardship both by the examples they set in leading and managing the congregation's resources and by how they speak of their vision for the church and the need of members to give.

The churches of my small-town childhood were modest in size, and were relatively new. Such congregations might expect the current membership to fund the needs of the program as well as the physical plant. However, even my boyhood church — now occupying a church over 125 years old and a Sunday school building approaching its centenary — has established an endowment to help with the capital maintenance of the increasingly historic buildings.

In many parts of the country, previous generations built large buildings of great architectural significance. These buildings are gifts not only to the congregation and the denomination, but to the surrounding community, and, in some spectacular instances, to the world. It is completely appropriate that the generation that gives a gift that requires maintenance and upkeep should endow the maintenance of their gift. Otherwise, the gift turns over time into an unaffordable liability. Universities have certainly understood this principle for many years, while many congregations seem just barely beginning to learn it. Again and again, one finds splendid buildings from the nineteenth century erected in the years before the income tax by prosperous congregations that failed to endow them. Perhaps they assumed that there would always be prominent people to make up the annual deficit or to fund needed improvements. Perhaps, then as now, people thought that new buildings simply wouldn't require maintenance. And perhaps they *were* once endowed, but the congregation has depleted the endowment either by overdrawing it or by failing to invest it so that it maintained its purchasing power over the years.

Some of the congregations with the most vital personal stewardship also have significant long-term investments. Congregations that treat their long-term investments prudently as one component of their health and life will leave to the next generation a stronger institution better empowered to carry on an effective Christian witness.

Some Cautionary Examples

Unfortunately, there are also many instances of congregational leaders who have not dealt well with their long-term investments. "You don't need to give," one priest told his congregation. "We can take it from the endowment." That priest's successor has had to work hard to revitalize the congregation's stewardship. It isn't difficult at all to convey the message that people don't have to give; your congregation will pick up on that message even when you haven't intentionally communicated it. It takes constant work and constant reinforcement to make good personal stewardship part of the ethos of a congregation.

Too many congregations use their long-term investments to make up any deficit that develops in the budget. Some congregations have put their future in serious jeopardy by spending down their long-term investments at an alarming rate. One congregation with several millions a generation ago found itself recently with less than $100,000. "Our long-term strategy," another finance committee chair said, "is to take whatever we need for the budget out of the investments."

During the mid-1990s, when the stock markets were rising rapidly, some congregations became accustomed to taking huge amounts out of their long-term investments every year. It seemed all right, since at the end of the year they had as much as they began with. Recent investment performance has not permitted these congregations to continue a practice they should never have adopted, precipitating a crisis that did not need to happen.

Who manages the portfolio is often a source of unease, if not outright conflict of interest. In one congregation, the portfolio was managed by a member of the investment committee who made over

$20,000 in transaction fees one year — nearly 3 percent of the value of the entire portfolio. In another congregation, the investment committee chair's broker handled the portfolio. Other members of the committee had concerns about his management, but were hesitant to raise questions for fear of offending the committee chair. You need an arm's-length manager whose performance you can frankly evaluate without causing a rift in the congregation.

No matter how your investments are managed, it is necessary for someone to calculate the return on the portfolio and present quarterly reports that compare the performance of the entire portfolio to agreed-on benchmarks. One congregation's long-term investments lost 40 percent of their value during a period when the markets were good, but no one was monitoring the performance. Another found that, because of the rise in the stock market, their portfolio was almost 100 percent in stocks because they hadn't been monitoring the allocation of the investments between equities and bonds as the stock market was rising.

Numerous congregations, thinking to avoid risk, have compromised their long-term investments by putting them all in fixed-income investments, like bonds or CDs, and then spending all their income. One congregation invested a large bequest in U.S. Treasury bonds in the late 1980s and drew all the income for a decade. They thought they were acting as prudent fiduciaries. In fact, they had both squandered what they had and missed one of the greatest rises in the history of the stock market during the 1990s. Taking into account the rate of inflation as calculated by the Bureau of Labor Statistics, the $800,000 they began with was worth about $581,000 in 1998 in constant dollars. And the decade in which they had buried this particular talent saw a tremendous rise in the stock market. You can't avoid risk; it will be either the risk of the equity markets or the risk of inflation.

Another congregation came to grief by investing in stocks the capital campaign funds they were planning to spend on building improvements within twenty-four months. When it came time to draw the money out, they had less than they started with because the stock market had dipped. Short-term reserve funds need a different strategy from long-term invested funds. Not-for-profit fiduciaries should not go for short-term stock market gains. The strategy for long-term investments has to be, well, long-term. You must be prepared to ride out market cycles.

Responsibilities of Fiduciaries

If your congregation owns its own assets, then the leaders entrusted with the oversight of those assets are fiduciaries. It isn't necessary to work on Wall Street to be a good fiduciary of your congregation's financial assets. Those who are responsible for the management and use of a congregation's long-term investments should welcome the opportunity to give a regular account of their stewardship. They should want to make sure the entire leadership understands how the funds are invested, why they are invested that way, how much is being used, and for what purpose. Other members should feel free to ask questions about these matters until they understand them.

In short, the investment committee or treasurer should give timely, easy-to-understand reports, and the members of the governing board should make the effort to understand the investment approach and the reports. There should be no mystification or abdication of responsibility, only transparency and mutual accountability.

That's easy to say, right? There are congregations where all this is happening, but there aren't as many as one might hope.

Some Dynamics You May Recognize

If my experience is any guide, the way investments are handled is far more likely to look like this: Once a quarter, the vestry receives a report on the investments. On a single page the treasurer tries to report on both each named fund and the securities held in the investment accounts. The report combines information usually found on the balance sheet with information appropriate for a revenue and expense statement. The result is a jumble of numbers with lots of columns and even more rows. The numbers can finally yield some information, but not very easily. The report is only in dollar amounts, so there are no performance calculations and no comparisons to benchmarks.

One of the reasons the reports are confusing is that the manager is handling several investment accounts. Though there may have been reasons for keeping certain funds separate, nobody is quite sure what those reasons were. As it is, each account is invested in different ways, and nobody pays much attention to the allocation of assets between equities and fixed-income funds. The dollar amounts of withdrawals are shown, but no one thinks of what is taken out as a percentage of the balance.

The treasurer always repeats that the report was difficult to design and is laborious to produce. The vestry does appreciate getting even information that's hard to understand because for many years the former treasurer, who insisted that an investment committee was unnecessary, did not report on the investments at all. However, most members don't feel they understand anything about the investments, and they're afraid to ask. The treasurer, aware that the report is not very clear, takes any questions as criticism and bristles accordingly. The treasurer responds in a way intended to convey that the questioner doesn't understand investments. Since most of the vestry in fact don't understand investments very well, they're now thoroughly cowed.

No one ever says anything in a meeting, but afterward in the parking lot several people regularly share their misgivings about the investment manager, a friend of the investment committee chair who took over the management after the former treasurer (finally) resigned. The former treasurer, one of the richest members of the congregation, managed the investments personally, and no one dared say a word. People suspect that the current manager gets a transaction fee every time something is bought or sold in the portfolio, but it's hard to say since the manager never attends a vestry meeting, and this possibly useful piece of information is completely hidden in the reports.

All these dynamics make the investment reports so fraught at vestry meetings that everyone tries to rush through them. Every so often, though, after the annual election there's a new member who tries to ask about the investment strategy, or the asset allocation, or how much is being used. It becomes necessary to figure out how to get the new member to know that while it's okay to ask such questions once (because it would be nice if somehow everybody felt a little more comfortable about how things are being managed), they shouldn't be repeated.

Last year, though, a member came on who couldn't take the hint, and refused to go along with not asking questions. A few people hoped that this might help break the logjam, but the new member just spars with the treasurer for a while. It has now become a contest of wills, and everyone breathes a sigh of relief when the latest exchange is over, although their unease and their unanswered questions remain.

If any of that sounds familiar, see if there's a way to organize your investments to minimize these dynamics. Sometimes you need a voice from outside the system to introduce needed reforms. Maybe this book can serve as that voice. Maybe your judicatory has a resource that can second the message. For the sake of the future of your congregation, please see that you get the help you need to put things in order if your congregation is handling your long-term investments poorly.

The existence of substantial, well-managed long-term investments can be a blessing to an active congregation and to the lives of those the congregation touches. Long-term investments are usually the result of bequests by previous generations. If the gifts of previous generations are handled well, your current members are more likely to remember your congregation in their wills. On the other hand, poor handling of long-term investments will make your members less likely to leave bequests to your congregation and can jeopardize the congregation's very existence. Use the expertise and resources available to help ensure the long-term health of your congregation.

Why Many Fail to Achieve Their Goals

Remember that you have two goals with respect to your long-term investments. The goals need to be achieved simultaneously. First, you want your long-term investments to maintain their purchasing power over time in constant dollars, so that their value will keep up with inflation. Second, you want to provide a reasonable and reasonably steady stream of funds from your investments to fund your current work. What follows are the considerations and practices aimed at allowing you to achieve both of these goals.

An experienced cook knows how to bring back together a sauce that has separated, whereas a beginner might throw it away and start over. An experienced skier will know how to deal with an unexpected irregularity in the terrain that might leave the beginner in a heap of broken bones. When we know what we're doing, we have some confidence in our skills. We can keep our eyes on the ultimate outcome, and we won't be distracted by temporary successes and failures. When we're unsure, we're likely to be driven by sudden fear or elation.

In general we fail as investors because we are unsure and allow our decisions to be dictated by the ups and downs of the markets. We take our eyes off the long-term horizon and make decisions to buy and sell based on the way the markets are moving right now. If we move with the herd, we buy what everyone else is buying and sell what everyone else is selling. This approach virtually guarantees that

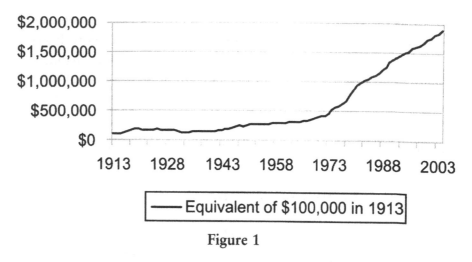

Figure 1

our investments will not perform as well as the markets themselves because we'll tend to buy what is already overvalued and sell when things are already near the bottom.

To do a good job with your investments you can't make decisions based on either panic or giddiness. Insulate yourself from your emotions by creating a structure and a policy to guide your decisions. You can't eliminate risk in investing, but you can manage risk. Keep your eye on your long-term objectives.

Many Parishes Forget about Inflation

Before World War I, although there were periods of inflation, the economy did not experience chronic inflation. In those days church endowments were typically held in bonds or other fixed-income investments like mortgages. If you ended up with the same amount of principal at the end of the year that you had at the beginning, that was all right, because in general the dollar was worth just as much on December 31 as it had been worth the previous January 1. It was appropriate and prudent to invest for income. As long as you didn't dip into the principal, you were doing fine.

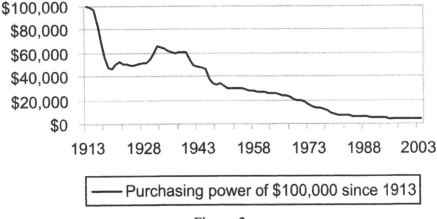

Figure 2

Since World War I, however, the story has been quite different. Inflation has averaged about 3.1 percent per year since 1913. This means that at the end of 2004 it took almost $1,900,000 to buy what $100,000 bought in 1913. The other way to look at the effect of inflation is to see how the purchasing power of the same number of dollars decreases. If you had carefully preserved the $100,000 principal your parish received in 1913, it would have been worth only $3,700 in constant dollars at the end of 2004. Figure 1 illustrates the nominal dollars you needed in 2004 to buy what $100,000 bought in 1913. Figure 2 shows how the purchasing power of $100,000 declined in constant dollars from 1913 through 2004. The figures are from the Bureau of Labor Statistics Web site (*www.bls.gov*).

Although for nearly a century chronic inflation has been part of the economy, many congregations still invest for income only, without taking inflation into account. Such a practice seems safe, but it accomplishes neither of the two goals that you must accomplish simultaneously if you are to be good stewards of your long-term investments.

For example, say you received $500,000 in 1993, which you invested in bonds that paid 6.6 percent. (On January 3, 1993, ten-year

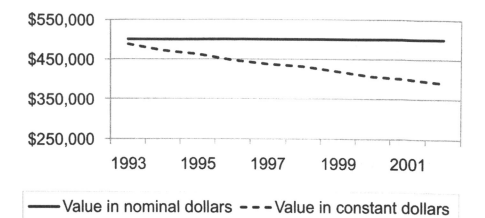

Figure 3

bonds were paying 6.6 percent.) That's $33,000 per year that you could count on. You have taken the $33,000 each year into your operating budget, and at the end of a ten-year period you still have the $500,000 and it has produced $330,000 for you over those ten years. What could be wrong with that?

Two things are wrong. The first is that, instead of maintaining the purchasing power of your investments with respect to inflation, you have allowed inflation to erode their value in constant dollars. By 2002 the value of the $500,000 you started with ten years earlier was about $389,700 in constant dollars (Figure 3). The second is that, instead of providing for a reasonable and reasonably steady stream of income every year for your purposes, you also are receiving less every year to use for your purposes. By the end of 2002 it took almost $41,100 to buy what the $33,000 bought in 1993. The final $33,000 in interest that you received in 2002 was the equivalent of $26,500 ten years earlier (Figure 4).

In other words, the two things wrong with handling your investments as in this example are that you failed to achieve both of your investment goals. You've allowed inflation both to erode the value of your investments and to diminish the amount they provide for

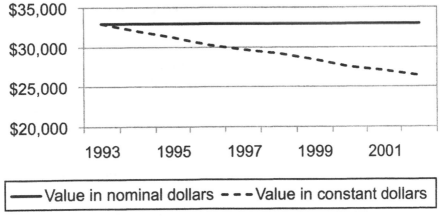

Figure 4

your current needs. There is certainly no long-term future down that dead-end road. The discussion that follows might help you avoid such common dead-ends. We'll revisit this congregation and its $500,000 later to see how things might have worked differently.

I keep harping on the effects of inflation because I keep encountering parishes — even those with several million in investments — that believe they are avoiding risk by investing 90 percent or more in bonds and drawing all the interest into their budgets. In a way, though, if this is how you invest, you *are* avoiding risk: there is no *risk* of inflation. There is the *certainty* of inflation. By investing for income and failing to account for inflation, you are trading the risk of the stock market's volatility for the certainty of inflation's erosive effects. It's as if you were selling 3 percent of your property every year. How much land would you have left if you did that for a couple of decades? If you are investing for income and drawing out all the income, I want to shatter the false sense of security you have. Over the long term, you can prudently use from your investments only what the portfolio earns *after* inflation. That brings us to the way most secular not-for-profits have been investing for a good many years now.

Total Return Investing

Investments produce two kinds of return: income (interest and dividends) and appreciation or depreciation (generally a rise or fall in the price of a share of stock, or capital gains and losses). Traditional not-for-profit investing policy said you should spend only income but put little emphasis on appreciation. Total return investing considers both income and appreciation as part of the return. All income and gains are reinvested, and the organization withdraws a percentage of the average balance without distinguishing whether the amount withdrawn is made up of "income" or "capital gains."

Fixed-income investments like mortgages and government and corporate bonds provide income, not capital appreciation. Although the principal value of bonds and mortgages fluctuate according to market conditions, the fundamental idea of fixed-income instruments is that if you hold the bond or mortgage from the time it is issued until it matures, you will receive a fixed rate of interest over the term of the instrument, and at the end you will get back exactly the same number of dollars as you invested.

Fixed-income instruments — especially those backed by government guarantees — feel safe because the interest rate is fixed, and the principal is guaranteed. However, inflation is the serpent in the apparent Eden of U.S. Treasuries and government-backed mortgages. At the end of the term you get back the same number of dollars you put in. You don't get more dollars to compensate for the effects of inflation.

While the return on bonds and mortgages is mostly income and not capital appreciation, the reverse is true of the return on stocks. Stocks typically pay little in terms of dividends. Most of the returns in the stock market come from increases in the value of the shares of stock — appreciation, or capital gains.

If you invest for income, you'll be likely to weight your portfolio toward investments that generate the highest rates of interest available, and you will likely draw all the income those investments produce, thus allowing the value of your portfolio to be eroded by inflation.

If you invest on a total return basis, you are not investing for "income"; you're investing for both income and appreciation. Gains, dividends, and interest together make up the total return you receive on your investments. You allocate your investments between equities (stocks) and fixed-income instruments both to spread the risk and to benefit from the returns in both kinds of investments. You reinvest everything the portfolio earns, instead of asking to receive the interest and dividends as they are earned. The amount you withdraw every year is a percentage of the average value of the investments.

Your two goals are (1) to maintain the purchasing power of your investments, and (2) to produce a reasonable stream of resources every year for your current purposes. Thus, your investment goal is for your investments over the long term to earn the rate of inflation plus the percentage you take out. Total return investing makes it more likely that you will achieve your goals because over the long term you will benefit from the returns of both the equity and fixed-income markets.

Diversification Helps Manage the Risks

You cannot *eliminate* risk from the management of investments. You can *manage* the risks, however, by diversifying your portfolio, that is, by allocating your assets among different kinds of investments. In general, investments that have a higher historical return have greater risk. You get paid extra for taking more risk. Total return investing allows you to manage the risks of investing by allocating your assets among different asset classes that have different levels of risk and return and that perform differently at any point in an economic cycle.

An asset class is a kind of investment. Within the broad categories of stocks and bonds there are many asset classes. The following paragraphs are meant only to acquaint you with some of the terms you hear investment professionals use. My purpose is not to overwhelm you, but to give you a sense that there are many ways to allocate your funds and thereby to manage your risks.

Stocks can be domestic (U.S.) or international. Some international stocks are those of the "emerging markets" (sometimes called the Third World). Companies come in different sizes, so investors speak of large-cap, mid-cap, and small-cap stocks, referring to different levels of market capitalization, that is, the total value of all the stock the company has issued. Though the limits vary, large-cap usually means companies with a market capitalization of $10 billion or more; mid-cap, $2 billion–$10 billion, and small-cap, less than $2 billion.

There are "value" stocks and "growth" stocks. A value stock is one in which the price of the stock in relation to its earnings is below the market average, so the company is considered undervalued. A value investor assumes that the market will discover and correct this error by bringing the stock price up to "where it belongs." If the sales and earnings of a company are growing faster than average, the stock is considered a growth stock. Because the company is doing so well, people will pay more for the stock even if the price of the stock in relation to its earnings is above the market average.

Investments are also spread over different sectors of the economy — for example, financial services, technology, health care, communications, utilities, real estate, and natural resources. At any point some sectors of the economy are performing better than others, and, of course, within a sector, certain companies will be doing better than others. Spreading your investments over different sectors is another way to manage risk.

There are also many kinds of fixed-income investments. U.S. Treasury notes, or T-notes, are issued in short or intermediate durations of two to ten years. They pay a fixed rate of interest every six months. A T-note will sell above or below its face value depending on the relationship between the bond's interest rate and prevailing rates. The U.S. Treasury stopped issuing Treasury bonds, or T-bonds, in October 2001. However, since T-bonds were issued for durations as long as thirty years, they will be on the market for many years. At this writing the federal government is set to reissue thirty-year bonds in February 2006. T-bonds pay a fixed rate of interest every six months and trade above or below their face value depending on market conditions. The Treasury also issues Treasury bills, or T-bills, that are short-term (less than a year) fixed-income securities.

Corporations also issue bonds. There are agencies that rate these bonds by assessing the credit-worthiness of the issuing entity. As we have seen, because the return on an investment increases with the risk, the lower the rating the bond receives, the riskier it is, and the higher the interest rate the issuer has to pay. More highly rated corporate bonds are called "investment grade," while those that are lower rated are called "high-yield." Governments and corporations have an incentive to keep their finances in good shape so they can borrow money by issuing bonds at a lower interest rate. Other fixed-income investments include mortgages and the debt of foreign governments and non-U.S. companies.

Real estate is another asset class. The real estate market moves independently of the stock market and the bond market. There are two ways to own real estate. You may own a house, an apartment building, or a commercial building that you rent out. If you own the property primarily to generate rental income, you'll want to consider that asset when you think of the total assets you have that generate a return. If the property is purely for investment purposes and is not part of your program space — that is, the church, parish house, parsonage, or education building — it's perfectly okay to consider whether you might get a better return if the property were converted to investments. If you own a rental property worth $250,000 and you have $400,000 in long-term investments, it means that nearly 40 percent of your total assets are in that house. If you're clearing less than 4 percent of the value in net rent after all the expenses, you might want to consider whether you'd be better off with that money in financial investments. Make sure you have the proper discipline and controls in place so you don't just spend the money if you do decide to sell the house.

Another way to own real estate is to invest in a REIT, a Real Estate Investment Trust. REITs function as kind of a mutual fund whose holdings are commercial real estate; often an REIT specializes in one kind of commercial real estate, like shopping malls. By owning shares of the REIT, you participate in the ownership of property with the advantage of being able to sell your holdings easily. You typically won't want more than 5 percent or 10 percent of your assets in such an investment.

Because there are so many possibilities, it is essential for you to have a plan and a structure for your investments so you don't go chasing after the most recent investment option someone was talking about on TV, or let your emotions tell you when to buy and sell. There are three ways to help you manage both the risks of the markets and the risks posed by your emotions.

1. Adopt investment guidelines.

Your investment guidelines can be simple. They outline your investment objectives, the target allocation of assets among the various classes that will achieve those objectives, the benchmarks to which you will compare your actual performance, and parameters for re-balancing. In adopting guidelines, you make the crucial decisions in advance based on historical performance and best practices. When the markets are moving up or down, your guidelines will help you be guided by your head, not by your churning stomach.

2. Use mutual funds.

You are the fiduciary of a perpetual institution. You are not a stock-picker or day-trader. Mutual funds give you both an arm's-length structure and a diversification you cannot achieve with a modest-sized portfolio of individual stocks. It's also usually cheaper for you to pay mutual fund fees than to put your portfolio with a manager who buys and sells stocks in your portfolio. Do not invest in individual stocks; use mutual funds with reasonable performance histories and low fees.

3. Don't depend on an individual.

There are two compelling reasons not to depend on one individual in your congregation to manage your portfolio. First, the investment horizon for your congregation is much longer than any individual's time on earth. If there is one person who is making your investment decisions, there is almost sure to be a succession problem, especially if that person has been doing it for some time. People who have been entrusted with the stewardship of a part of parish life tend to begin to act as if they own that piece of parish turf, and that always has negative consequences. This outcome is less likely to occur if a group rather than a single individual is made responsible for something. If you have just one person doing it, look for an opportunity to change that. If your judicatory or denomination offers an investment service to its congregations, I strongly recommend that you consider using it. Perhaps the member of your congregation who is so good with investments could offer his or her services best by serving on the board or committee that oversees your judicatory's investment program.

You can't eliminate risk of the markets; you mustn't ignore the relentless effects of inflation; and you need to create a buffer between your emotional responses and your management of your investments. However, you don't need to feel buffeted or pulled by these conflicting forces. You can steer a steady and rational course.

Determining the Asset Mix

Your investment goal is a function of what you want to earn above inflation and your tolerance for market risk. The more aggressive models have a higher rate of return over time, but the ride might be a little more exciting than you like. On the other hand, if you opt for a model with lower risk, you will be able to take less out every year to fund your mission.

The percentage you can prudently take out depends on how you've allocated your assets between stocks and bonds. From 1952 through 2004 stocks have produced on average a return of about 11.4 percent per year before inflation, or a "real return" (that is, after inflation) of about 7.5 percent. Inflation in the same period has been about 4 percent per year. In the same period, fixed-income investments have produced a rate of return of 7 percent before inflation, for a real rate of return of 3 percent. Therefore, if the portfolio is invested 60 percent in equities and 40 percent in fixed-income securities, the average real return will be roughly 5 percent, after taking into account both inflation and about 0.75 percent for investment management fees. The calculations I've used can be seen on the Web site that accompanies this book (*www.churchpublishing.org/rememberthefuture*).

A number of universities and other not-for-profits with significant investments have lowered the percentage they draw down every year to 4 percent or 4.5 percent plus fees. Regardless of the allocation of your assets, probably any amount that you take out of your investments that exceeds 5 percent plus fees must be considered overdrawing your investments.

The percentage you can take out is determined by the allocation of your assets. If you are 80 percent in bonds and only 20 percent in stocks, the percentage you can take out will be more like 2.5 percent after accounting for inflation and fees. Calculating your takeout as a percentage of your assets rather than "whatever we need" is certainly a step in the right direction, but it is crucial to let the percentage be set by the historical return of your asset allocation model.

Strategic or Tactical Approach

Investment advisors talk about taking either a strategic or tactical approach to managing investments. Both approaches assume the principles and practices of total return investing, but there are differences in the execution.

A strategic investor will concentrate on maintaining the target asset allocation. If the policy calls for 60 percent equities and 40 percent fixed-income investments, the strategic investor will rebalance within fairly narrow bands. If a rise in the stock market causes the allocation to change to 66 percent stocks and 34 percent bonds, the strategic investor will rebalance to the target. The strategic investor takes the position that the goal will be achieved by maintaining the asset allocation through the ups and downs of market cycles.

The tactical investor will have a long-term asset allocation model but will allow much greater flexibility in what the actual mix might be, depending on market conditions. The long-term model might still be 60 percent stocks/40 percent bonds, but the actual allocation in the portfolio might look very different at various points in the market cycle. However, the successful tactical investor's asset mix will likely be the reverse of the conventional wisdom of the amateur investor. In 1999, when the stock market was nearing its peak, many people were weighted heavily toward stocks because of how quickly they were rising, and many of these people were caught short when the markets started to fall in March 2000. The successful tactical investor would have been selling stocks throughout that period of "irrational exuberance," so at the top of the market that tactical portfolio would have likely have been less than 50 percent stocks. In the down years of 2001 and 2002, when many investors had gotten completely out of the stock market, the tactical investor would have been buying stocks. When the market began to turn up in 2003, the successful tactical investor might have been 70 percent or more in stocks.

Both the strategic and the tactical approaches invest against the market, selling stocks as they rise and buying them when they are down. However, the tactical investor's range is considerably greater than that permitted by the strategic approach. The strategic investor tends to think that the tactician veers too close to market timing, which means thinking that you can predict ups and downs with more precision than anyone can have. The tactical investor tends to think that the strategist acts with a wooden rigidity that ignores obvious developments in the market. If you have a couple of professionals on your investment committee who take the different sides of this debate, you'll have some interesting (though, for you, largely incomprehensible) meetings.

If anything I have said in this chapter has been at all new for you, and if you have responsibility for managing your congregation's investments, I think you will want to adopt the strategic approach. If you don't have access to an investment program managed by your judicatory or denomination, I think you'll want to set a basic asset allocation model, and rebalance when it ends a quarter outside the target range you set as part of your model.

Figuring the Moving Average

Once you have determined the asset allocation and the resulting percentage you can take out, you compute the amount you can withdraw from the portfolio by multiplying the percentage by the average value of the investments. Averaging smoothes the ups and downs of the market, making your income stream less volatile. There are two common ways of computing the average value of the portfolio: either a three-year moving average or a twelve- or thirteen-quarter moving average.

The three-year method means averaging the market value of the investments at the same date for the previous three years. Most of the time the date is December 31, but if you make it September 30, you'll know what the drawdown will be as you make the next year's budget. You calculate how much you can take out in the following year by multiplying that average value by your percentage rate. The amount of the 2006 drawdown will be your percentage multiplied by the average of the values on December 31 or September 30 of 2003, 2004, and 2005. For 2007 you'd drop the 2003 value and add the 2006 value. In the example below, the annual drawdown comes to $56,464. The quarterly installments would be $14,116.

Balance at 9/30/03	$1,036,255
Balance at 9/30/04	1,223,090
Balance at 9/30/05	1,128,477

$3,387,822 ÷ 3 = $1,129,274 × 5% = **$56,464**

The thirteen-quarter average for the first quarter of 2006 would be found by averaging the value at the end of every quarter from December 31, 2002, through December 31, 2005. For the second quarter drop the December 31, 2002, number and add the value at March 31, 2006. Because you're calculating only one-quarter of your drawdown, you multiply the thirteen-quarter average by 1.25 percent, or multiply by 5 percent and divide by 4.

Balance at 12/31/02	$1,231,161
Balance at 3/31/03	1,213,095
Balance at 6/30/03	1,135,271
Balance at 9/30/03	1,036,255
Balance at 12/31/03	1,050,935
Balance at 3/31/04	1,017,918
Balance at 6/30/04	1,100,678
Balance at 9/30/04	1,223,090
Balance at 12/31/04	1,160,693
Balance at 3/31/05	1,163,134
Balance at 6/30/05	1,151,317
Balance at 9/30/05	1,128,477
Balance at 12/31/05	1,303,340

$$\$14,915,364 \div 13 = 1,147,366 \times 1.25\% = \mathbf{\$14,342}$$

Buying Low and Selling High

The goal of all investors is to buy at the bottom of the market before prices start to rise and to sell at the top before the market starts to fall. That's what everyone wants to do, but it is always unclear at any moment in the markets when the top or the bottom has been reached. Not only is it difficult to know where you are in a market cycle, buying low and selling high means investing against the current market trends. When it seems that stocks can go only up, that's when the professionals are moving funds out of the stock market to conserve the gains they've made. When the amateurs are rushing out of the stock market because it's falling, that's when the same professionals are moving into stocks so they'll be there when the market turns.

Maintaining a target asset allocation between stocks and bonds not only allows you to spread the risks and benefits of the stock and bond markets, it also provides a rough but reliable way of preserving the gains you've made in one part of the market and investing in the other part when prices are low. In other words, maintaining your asset allocation more or less forces you to invest against the markets. In order to maintain the target allocation, you sell stocks when stocks are up to buy bonds. If the stock market has gone down, maintaining your asset allocation means putting funds into a weak stock market.

Say you are maintaining a 60 to 40 percent allocation between stocks and bonds with a $1,000,000 portfolio. Say the next year in the stock market was a good one, with a return of 26 percent, while the bond market was down a bit with a total return including interest of 1 percent. The $600,000 you had in stocks has grown by 26 percent to $756,000, while the bond portion is $404,000. Your portfolio is now worth $1,160,000. Your asset allocation is now 65 percent stocks and 35 percent bonds. Rebalancing now would mean moving about $60,000 from stocks to bonds in order to return to the target allocation. You start the next year with a 60/40 allocation, but the new figures arc $696,000 in stocks and $464,000 in bonds.

	Stocks	%	Bonds	%	Total
At January 1	600,000	60%	400,000	40%	1,000,000
At December 31	756,000	65%	404,000	35%	1,160,000
After rebalancing	696,000	60%	464,000	40%	1,160,000

The discipline of the target allocation means that you have taken a fair amount of what you earned in a rising stock market and have conserved those gains by rebalancing. You have just sold high and bought low.

Some Ways It Can Work

Let's revisit the parish that received $500,000 in 1993. They invested 100 percent in ten-year Treasury notes. On January 4, 1993, ten-year bonds were being issued at 6.6 percent. The treasurer was delighted to know that the budget would be receiving exactly $33,000 every year for the next ten years. Sure, there was some criticism as the stock market rose so high for the rest of the 1990s, but those critics were silenced when the stock market began to fall in the spring of 2000.

Here is the way the treasurer reported on his stewardship of the assets at the annual meeting in January 2003:

1. A total of $330,000 for the parish budget over a ten-year period when interest rates hit near-historic lows; and

2. The original $500,000 still in the safekeeping of the parish.

However, because of the effects of inflation, by the end of 2002 you needed $622,500 to have the equivalent of $500,000 at January 1993. Moreover, by January 2003, interest rates were down, and ten-year bonds were paying 4.07 percent, so now the parish could look forward to receiving $20,350 in interest. This is equivalent to only $15,981 in 1993 dollars.

So the real story is that the $500,000 has been significantly depleted by inflation, and the income the parish will receive going forward will be less than half of what they received in 1993.

Let's compare those results with what would have happened if the treasurer had invested in two index funds, that is, mutual funds that own the same holdings as are computed in the major benchmark indices. The returns in an index fund track the return of the index, and the fees are very low. We'll assume fees of 0.25 percent of the balance annually. We'll also assume that the investment guidelines of the parish called for 60 percent of the portfolio in an S&P 500 index fund and 40 percent in a mutual fund that tracks the Lehman Aggregate

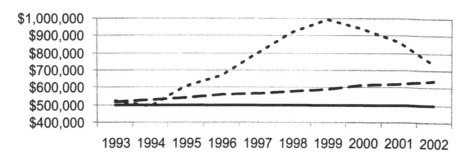

Figure 5

index, one of the major indices for the fixed-income markets. The guidelines call for a rebalancing of the portfolio to the 60 percent/40 percent level whenever the actual allocation varies by more than 5 percent. Thus, if the stock fund represented more than 65 percent or less than 55 percent of the portfolio, the funds would be rebalanced to the target of 60 percent/40 percent.

At the end of 2002, after several years of very good returns in the 1990s and three years of down markets in which many people lost a great deal, our test parish would have $746,000 invested (Figure 5). Over the ten-year period, they would have drawn down $349,000 plus the fees. They would have started drawing down $25,000, but by 2002 the drawdown would have been $47,145 (Figure 6).

I invite readers to check the Web site that accompanies this book for more information (*www.churchpublishing.org/rememberthefuture*). While the period I selected included one of the biggest run-ups in the stock market in history, it also included three years of heavy losses for many people, and the period ends at the bottom of the bear market. The fact is that for almost any ten-year period since the end of World War II, the story would be similar: a portfolio handled as suggested here at least keeps up with inflation. It is not true of every period, however. In the 1970s the U.S. economy experienced sluggish

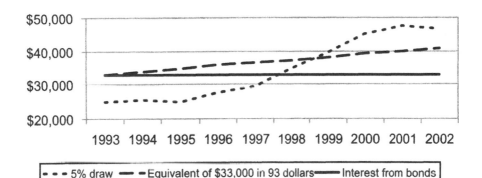

Figure 6

economic growth with high inflation and high interest rates. However, even then, over the long term, a restrained and disciplined investment strategy would have paid off.

Report and Monitor

If you are handling your own investments, I counsel you to avoid negligence on the one hand and obsessive behavior on the other. If you are using index funds or other mutual funds, and assuming that you are adhering to an asset allocation model, then relax a little. Report on the investments to the governing board only quarterly. The board should of course receive a monthly budget report, but *do not* report on the investments every month. Such frequent reports on the investments will serve no good purpose; on the contrary, such frequent reporting will serve only to increase everyone's anxiety even if the market is rising. Anxiety drives out leadership, so don't be part of that dynamic.

If you are the one reporting, and you still think it's important to report monthly, you might want to do a little self-examination. Being the bearer of news that increases anxiety makes you the center of attention and gives you a kind of control in the group. Be alert to the possibility that you might be motivated by some such inner need, and seek God's help to change. In one parish the treasurer wanted everything in bonds. When the investment committee decided to make a small investment in an equity mutual fund, the treasurer made sure he reported at every vestry meeting on the movement of the fund. Whether the fund had gone up or down, the anxiety was palpable. It didn't take long for the vestry to vote to sell the holding. Report on the investments quarterly.

When you report, the dollar activity is less important than the percentage change compared to your benchmarks. An increase of $40,000 or a loss of $100,000 is not meaningful unless it is put into context. The context is always the answer to these two questions: (1) What was the quarterly and year-to-date performance of our investments in percentage terms? and (2) How does that performance compare to our benchmarks?

If you have an investment advisor for your portfolio, or if you are in a managed fund offered by your judicatory or denomination, you should be receiving such reports. If, like many parishes, you have several small investment accounts with different managers, you need to calculate the total return of the whole portfolio taken together so you can make adequate reports to the board. You have to account for additions and withdrawals, and you have to account for reinvested income. And make sure you include the performance of the benchmarks. From the Web site accompanying this book (*www.churchpublishing.org/rememberthefuture*) you can download a spreadsheet that will help you do all this easily.

If the board has a target asset allocation model, don't be obsessive about rebalancing. A common practice is to rebalance when the actual allocation has diverged 5 percent or more from the target. Sometimes you may go several years without rebalancing. Other times you may need to rebalance more frequently.

A Summary of Points to Remember

1. Bear in mind that a congregation is a perpetual institution.

As fiduciaries, the congregation's leaders must look to the longest possible horizon. Your congregation has a future. You must plan for it. In this country we have congregations that are over three hundred years old. In parts of the country there are numerous pre-Revolutionary War buildings. Who could have imagined then what we take for granted now? We need to manage what we now have so that our successors one hundred or two hundred years from now will thank us for our wise and prudent leadership.

2. Remember – your permanent assets are the land you own and your long-term investments.

Make sure you treat your long-term investments as a perpetual asset. We've been talking mostly about handling the money itself, but remember that your long-term investments are part of your total assets, and you need to manage all your assets as part of a long-term vision for the future. And your management of one part of your assets affects your members' response to other initiatives. As we will see in chapter 6, there is a clear relationship between how you manage your investments and the success of any planned giving effort. I recommend that you treat all bequests and other planned gifts as permanent assets. That bequest is the last gift that a parishioner is going to give you. Hold onto it. Add it to your permanent investment pool. Invest it in such a way that it will maintain its purchasing power over time. A "policy" of hoping that people will die so you can make up the shortfall in your budget or take care of deferred maintenance is a shortsighted one. People do not want to see their final gifts used that way, and they'll stop leaving you bequests. Make it a fundamental assumption of your leadership and management that you will endeavor to maintain your perpetual assets in perpetuity.

3. Decide which of your financial assets are long-term investments and which are short-term reserve funds that you plan to spend in the near- or mid-term.

Long-term investments require a different investment strategy from short-term reserve funds. In order to achieve both of your goals with your long-term investments you *must* have a percentage of them in the stock market. Because you're taking the long view with these funds, you can ride out the market cycles. However, in order to have your reserve funds available to you when you need to spend them, you *must not* expose your short-term reserves to the possible downturns in the markets.

When I begin a discussion with parish leaders about their investments, I always ask that the treasurer prepare a list of all the money the congregation holds. The list needs to show where the money is held (brokerage account, CD, savings account, etc.) and what the leadership thinks the money is for (organ fund, operating reserves, rectory endowment, etc.). Then we try to figure out whether each fund is a long-term investment or a reserve fund. When I began having these meetings, I thought this would be a simple classification that everyone already agreed on, but it usually proves to be the longest part of the discussion. For example, the people around the table understand different things when they see "Organ Fund." Some think of it as a reserve fund that was started in order to replace or to maintain the organ. Others see it as an endowment fund, the income from which is to be used for the maintenance of the instrument or toward the support of the music program.

In order to decide how such a fund is to be invested, you must decide whether it is a reserve fund or a long-term invested fund. You just can't have it both ways. Here's what happens when you try to have it both ways. You put the money in some kind of fixed-income investment (CD, money market account, bond fund), and you draw all the income. As we have already seen, this is the worst of all worlds. If the fund is really a reserve fund that you're planning to spend, then you should keep it in some fixed-income vehicle, but you should reinvest the interest and allow the income to accumulate in the fund. That's how you maintain the value of the reserve fund with respect to inflation while you're waiting to accumulate all the contributions you need in order to proceed with the project. If the fund is really a long-term invested fund, then by investing for income and drawing all of it you're allowing inflation to erode the value of the principal and to diminish the amount available to you every year.

4. Pool all your long-term investments.

You don't need to keep your funds in many separate accounts. The bigger the pool, the easier it is to maintain your target asset allocation. You can easily track the individual named funds in the pool. On the Web site accompanying this book (*www.churchpublishing.org/ rememberthefuture*) I have provided the prototype of a very simple spreadsheet that allows you both to allocate income and gains and losses across the funds and to track the additions and withdrawals in each of the funds you would like to track. Close your separate accounts and pool them all together. You won't lose track of donor restrictions or of the value of each fund, and you'll make it possible to make better investment decisions because you won't be caught up in the details of many small accounts.

5. Think "total return."

Don't think in terms of "interest and dividends" versus "capital gains." That approach can distort your strategy by encouraging instruments that yield high "income" but no capital appreciation, thus compromising the purchasing power of the principal over the long term.

6. Figure your spending rate from your long-term investments based on your asset allocation.

Over the long run, the percentage you spend for current needs should not exceed the total return of the portfolio less inflation, which has averaged 3.1 percent over the last seventy-five years. The percentage you set must be based on the historical returns of the asset classes in your allocation. For example, a 60 percent equity/40 percent fixed-income allocation has returned, from 1952 through 2004, 5 percent above inflation and management fees. If you have only 20 percent in stocks, you can't take out 5, or even 4, percent.

7. *Adopt investment guidelines.*

These can be very, very simple. Adopting guidelines just means that you have thought through all the questions and agreed on the way you will handle your long-term investments. The guidelines you adopt should at least reference the following:

a. Your time horizon. This should be longer than ten years.

b. Your investment objectives. This is the target total return you are aiming for. Often the number is expressed as something like "9 percent before fees and inflation," or "CPI + 6 percent," meaning the change in the Consumer Price Index plus the real return before fees.

c. The asset classes you will use in the allocation.

d. The target asset allocation between equities, fixed-income instruments, and cash that will permit you to achieve your investment objectives. Commonly the target allocation to stocks is set somewhere between 50 and 70 percent, with the remainder in fixed-income investments.

e. The benchmarks to which you will compare the performance of your investments, for example, the S&P 500 or the Lehman Aggregate.

f. Rebalancing procedures. What will trigger a rebalancing of the portfolio?

If you can invest with your judicatory or denomination in a managed vehicle that maintains the asset allocation, reinvests, and calculates your drawdown and sends it to you, then you don't need investment guidelines. You just need a vote of the governing board to put all your long-term investments in that vehicle. If such a vehicle is available to you, it's probably best to use it.

8. Use mutual funds.

Even an equity portfolio of more than $1 million cannot give you sufficient diversification if you invest in individual stocks. Use mutual funds with good track records and reasonable fees that invest in areas that meet your goals. Perhaps your judicatory or denomination has an investment vehicle. If not, you might consider index funds. These mutual funds are designed simply to track the major benchmark indices. Because there are no management decisions, the fees are usually lower than other mutual funds or managed portfolios. Your returns will differ from the return of the index only by the amount of the fees.

9. Calculate your spending from your portfolio as a percentage of a moving average.

Use either a three-year moving average, by taking the average total value of the portfolio on the same date in three consecutive years, or the previous twelve or thirteen quarters.

10. Get an arm's-length manager.

Don't hire anyone to manage your portfolio whom you can't fire without causing a fuss. Avoid conflicts of interest and related party transactions. Do not have either a member of your congregation or a member's friend manage your investments. Your investment committee should oversee the manager, but the manager should be an outsider. If you have access to an investment service managed by your judicatory or denomination, by all means use it.

11. Monitor performance.

The governing board needs to know every quarter how the long-term investments are performing. The reports you receive from the managers might not give you the combined total return for the portfolio. In that case, you need to calculate total return, adjusting for additions, including reinvested income, withdrawals, and fees. Be sure you present the reports with comparisons to the benchmarks you have selected as reference points. If you are on the governing board, be sure to ask questions — gently but persistently — until you understand. That's your job.

12. Add to the principal.

Investments aren't just a legacy from the past, and they don't grow only by good performance in the markets. Leaders will want to add to the principal to strengthen further the future capabilities of the congregation. It's a good idea to try to add 1 percent to the principal every year in new gifts. You may not be able to add new funds every year. However, there are several things you can do that probably will result over time in significant new funds for your long-term investments. I suggest in chapter 6 that you treat all bequests as principal contributions to the investments, and in that chapter I discuss planned giving efforts and building the trust that is necessary so your members will make bequests and planned gifts to your congregation. Plan to make principal contributions to your investments over time that will average at least 1 percent per year.

13. Get the help you need.

Perhaps you don't have much investment expertise in-house. Perhaps the expertise you have is all in one rather domineering personality, or in one member's friend who is functioning as your broker. Perhaps you have several people who have lots of experience with investments but who have very different investment philosophies, so your investment committee has reached an impasse. If you have any unease about how the investments are being handled, please call on outside help. Ask your judicatory or your denominational headquarters to counsel you. Ask your colleagues in other congregations how they are managing. You owe it to your successors to do your best to get it right. And you're not alone.

14. Think of your long-term investments as one more limited stream of income.

Individual giving, fund-raising, and space-use income are all limited streams of income. What you can budget from these sources is limited. What you take from your long-term investments must also be limited to a prudent drawdown based on your asset allocation. And I say this for two reasons: (1) you need to limit what you use from the investments to preserve the purchasing power of the capital over time; and (2) you must also limit what you take from your investments so that you don't impair or undermine the personal stewardship of your members. I address this second point in more detail in chapter 6.

Conclusion

Managing investments, perhaps more than managing any other asset, makes us "deeply aware of the shortness and uncertainty of human life" (BCP, p. 504). There is no way to eliminate risk; it can only be managed. The performance of your investments depends not only on the management decisions you make, but on economic conditions. For example, from the late 1960s through the early 1980s the stock market was sluggish, and inflation was very high. During that period most portfolios couldn't have made the target of "inflation + drawdown and fees." According to the models you'll find on the Web site accompanying this book (*www.churchpublishing.org/rememberthefuture*), it would have taken until the early 1990s for portfolios to catch up. However, they would have caught up and then some, more than maintaining their purchasing power with regard to inflation.

Past performance, as we know, is no guarantee of future results. Therefore, please remember two things even as you do your best to implement and follow the investment practices discussed here.

First, do not develop an overreliance on your investments. If you rely too much on your investments, you will undoubtedly undermine the sense of responsibility your current members need for supporting the work of the congregation. Then, if management decisions or economic conditions cause your investments to lose some of their purchasing power, you will be caught short. The congregation will not be prepared to make up the shortfall because they will be accustomed to assuming that "other people's money" will carry the freight. If you realize that you are depending on your investments for too much of your operating budget, begin making a plan to reduce this dependence so your budget has a healthier shape. Chapter 6 is intended to help with this.

Second, I want to emphasize what I've said about adding to the principal. Your congregation needs to know that you are managing the investments prudently and exercising an appropriate restraint in using the resources they produce. Your members will respond to your planned giving efforts more willingly, and you will be forming in them the awareness that endowments are not only legacies from the past. Every generation has an important role in strengthening the congregation for the long-term future.

Chapter 4

Building Maintenance
for the Long Term

These stones that have echoed their praises are holy
And dear is the ground where their feet have once trod....

— "In our day of thanksgiving one psalm let us offer,"
William Henry Draper

Lord, I love the house in which you dwell
and the place where your glory abides.

—Psalm 26:8

The church is people, not buildings. The church is always the worshiping assembly of people, not the place where they gather. St. Paul knew nothing of church buildings; the congregations he knew met in members' houses. A few generations later, however, congregations had buildings, usually converted houses, that were exclusively used for the purposes of the congregation. Church buildings have since become so closely identified with the word "church" that members of Confirmation and Inquirers' classes are often surprised to learn that the church is people, not buildings.

However, almost all congregations have physical plants — often both venerable and extensive — in which to worship, to learn, to share fellowship, and to conduct parish and community programs. The focus of this chapter is on maintaining the fabric of your buildings.

Why Keep Up the Buildings?

Christ certainly did not "come only to teach us how to build handsome churches," as Bishop Henry Codman Potter of New York
pointed out in the late nineteenth century, when many of the most
handsome churches across the nation were being built. And some
Christians have accused others of having an "edifice complex." The
charge is no doubt unfair. For practicing Christians the church building is a place that is understandably important. It's where we've
celebrated significant life events and where we've made close friends
and see them regularly. Very likely it's where we've spent many hours
in fellowship and volunteer work, cooking, studying, talking, rak-
ing, and cleaning. Most important, the church building is where we
have encountered God. We've prayed and sung; we've been forgiven,
and we've learned to practice forgiveness. Of course, the building has
many layers of meaning for us.

The meaning and ties we have to the building don't necessarily
depend on its grandeur. In many a plain and humble church building
I've heard members say, "It's beautiful, isn't it?" And I always agree,
because that building is beautiful to those who worship there, as the
house in which I was raised was beautiful to my mother. When she
sold it after thirty-one years, she said that it was difficult to let go of,
not because it was anything so special, but because she had washed,
vacuumed, papered, painted, and cared for every board and every
corner of it again and again. She loved it as people love a place that
is full of memories and that they know deeply with their bodies.

This love does not depend on architectural merit and can be lav-
ished on places that are in dilapidated condition. Nevertheless, there
are at least two cogent reasons that the leaders of congregations
should properly maintain the buildings they own.

First, there is the fiduciary responsibility to the past and to the
future. Our buildings are part of our legacy from past generations.

The buildings permit the congregation to worship and to conduct programs and ministries. It is unfair to future generations not to pass them on in usable condition so that our successors will be able to use them for the work of Christ and the church in the world.

Part of the fiduciary responsibility is the realization that it is cheaper in the long run to keep buildings up and not to defer maintenance. It may cost your generation more than is easy for you to come up with, but it will cost the next generation much less because you've taken care of problems while they were small. We'll say much more about this.

Second, there is our responsibility to the present. Our buildings should not be eyesores or unusable. Years ago an elderly woman who had been raised by her Victorian grandmother articulated the best "theology of appearances" I've ever heard. "You have a duty to others," her grandmother had often admonished her, "to look as well as you can." We have a duty — to members, newcomers, visitors, occasional users of the buildings, passersby, neighbors, and the communities in which the buildings are located — to care for our buildings and grounds.

How well we fulfill this duty to others speaks volumes about us. Years ago, when I first visited a little church in a neighboring diocese, the congregation's self-image was perfectly mirrored in the dingy, overgrown appearance of the property. As soon as the people felt the congregation had a future, their sense of new life was immediately reflected in fresh paint and trimmed shrubbery. We have a duty to others to look as well as we can, and this duty is easier to fulfill if we have a sense of self-worth and some confidence in the future.

There is another aspect to our duty to the present beyond the appearance. Churches are public buildings. Our services of worship are open to the public, and most of us would like more of the public to attend them. We also use our buildings for concerts, meetings, and other public gatherings. We have a responsibility to invite the public into spaces that are not only well-kept, but safe. The public has the right to expect that any public building is reasonably maintained and safe. Governments have laws and building codes expressly designed to assure a minimum level of safety. Too many religious leaders think religious buildings should be exempted from these basic standards, and local governments are sometimes wary of citing religious institutions for violations. It does not speak well of either our self-esteem or our concern for others when we try to be exempted from standards that apply to everyone else. And the more inaccessible our buildings are — either by physical obstacles that hinder entrance or by failing to keep up with changing standards — the more marginalized we make ourselves. Your church may well be the only public building you ever enter that is not air conditioned; perhaps that helps explain why so many others are not entering it.

The proper maintenance of the buildings can seem overwhelming. What follows are ideas to help organize the job and break it down into manageable chunks so that the leadership can discharge its responsibilities with regard to the buildings.

Get Used to Thinking about It

The first thing to recognize about buildings is that they demand regular capital maintenance, not just the incidental maintenance of replacing light bulbs and fixing a broken faucet. With buildings, nothing is forever. Our hymnody says this more succinctly than any prose:

> Mortal pride and earthly glory,
>   sword and crown betray our trust;
> though with care and toil we build them,
>   tower and temple fall to dust.

> — "All my hope on God is founded,"
> *The Hymnal 1982,* 665

Everything in the buildings will have to be replaced, restored, or tended to, in regular cycles depending on the useful life of the component. A slate roof may last a hundred years or more; the kitchen and bathrooms need renovations much more frequently. And, as we will see, regular maintenance of nearly every system and element in our buildings is necessary in order for those components to last as long as they're meant to.

Leaders often profess to be caught by surprise by the failure of the boiler. However, the fact that a boiler has lasted fifty years does not mean it will last forever; rather, it means that it's near the end of its useful life. Don't be surprised if it breaks down this year.

Church leaders must accustom themselves to the idea that their buildings require regular, significant infusions of cash. As leaders accustom themselves to the idea that the buildings will not maintain themselves, they need not despair. They must simply plan accordingly.

Capital Replacement, Capital Maintenance, and Capital Repair

Let's get clear about what is involved.

Capital replacement

Every system and virtually every element in your buildings will have to be replaced. Each of these systems and elements has a useful life that is knowable. If you know that a Vermont slate roof was installed in 1925 and you're maintaining it properly, you need to be prepared to replace it around 2025. An asphalt shingle roof installed twenty years ago will require replacement in ten to twenty years. The boiler, the water heater, the electrical wiring, the plumbing pipes — everything has a useful life that you can estimate in order to make plans to replace it when the time comes.

A good many "emergencies" do not actually qualify for that appellation. They're not emergencies that could not have been foreseen; they're simply the predictable failure of a component that reached the end of its useful life — a life whose span was no secret or mystery. Everything needs replacement someday. Make it your business to know when so that you can make prudent provision for its replacement. Capital replacement shouldn't be a surprise; it can be planned for.

Capital maintenance

Most systems will need regular capital maintenance in order to achieve their full life span. For example, the exterior wood around your windows can last over two hundred years, but *only* if it is maintained and painted every seven to ten years. If you let the wood go unpainted, you reduce its useful life by 90 percent. The granite of your walls has a functional perpetual life, but the mortar holding the stone in place doesn't. You need to repoint when the mortar begins to weaken, and the mortar will give out decades sooner if you don't maintain the system of gutters and leaders that carry the water away from the buildings. To get the full life of your roof you need to replace missing slates or shingles, keep the flashing in good repair, keep the fascias painted, and maintain the gutters and leaders.

By the way, if someone tries to tell you that a product is "no-maintenance" and that it "will last a lifetime," you'd better start counting the silver. Everything needs some kind of attention to keep it in good repair, and the lifetime of your congregation that you have to plan for is a whole lot longer than any individual's time on earth. Since there is no such thing as a component that will last for hundreds of years with no maintenance, those aren't the criteria you should be using. Rather, you should be asking whether the material or method is appropriate to the structure, cost-effective over the long run, and time-proven. In a fair comparison on these criteria, traditional materials will usually come out ahead of more recent ones. The sales pitch fifty years ago may have been that aluminum siding would "last a lifetime." Now we know how long a lifetime is, and it's time to replace it. You might be better off re-siding the building with whatever the original material was.

Every building regardless of its age needs capital maintenance. A small congregation spoke to me of its plans to build a parish house. Since the congregation was struggling to maintain the century-old church building, I asked how they would maintain the new building. "Oh, a new building won't need maintenance," a leader replied. Down the path of this kind of wishful thinking lies nothing but more deferred maintenance.

Capital maintenance can and must be planned for. Failing to do proper upkeep (that is, deferring maintenance) is not "saving money"; it's just borrowing from the future.

Capital repair

Even with proper maintenance, it sometimes happens that a major system or element fails before the end of its expected life. These situations are by definition more difficult to predict because they involve, say, a boiler that fails before it should have. There may be manufacturers' warranties or other guarantees that will make good the repair. Sometimes there may not be. Your plans for capital reserve funds or the budget must make provision for unexpected capital repairs.

However, most surprises can be avoided if you are doing proper capital maintenance in an orderly way. The plastering and painting you had to do to the nursery after the big rainstorm wouldn't have been necessary if the rotted fascia had been replaced. And the fascia wouldn't have rotted if you'd just kept the gutters and leaders connected and cleaned. Regular maintenance of the small things can prevent most capital repairs.

Now that you're used to the idea that you have to keep up the buildings because they won't do it themselves, and now that we're clear on the kinds of things involved, here are some tips to help you keep the buildings under control.

Look Around Regularly

The best way not to be caught short by building problems is simply to inspect all the buildings regularly. Walk around and look. Inside and out. From the roof to the basement. And for the sake of heaven — and for the sake of the pastor and his or her family — don't forget the rectory or parsonage.

Is there any loose flashing? Are the gutters being cleaned at least twice a year? Are all the leaders connected to the gutters? Are they draining far enough from the foundation? Why is that paint peeling on the nursery wall? Is water getting in? What needs a minor repair? What needs to be replaced?

Make a list, and follow it up.

Then look around again in three months.

Get It While It's Small

Everything wears out or needs sprucing up eventually, but the most severe building problems come from water getting where it ought not to be. Some years ago the chair of our diocesan property support committee told a gathering of lay leaders that the main rule of building maintenance is, "Keep the water out!" It's called "sealing the envelope" — keeping the skin of the building (roof, flashing, exterior walls, windows, foundations) intact so that water can't get in.

Everywhere it finds a way — bad flashing, missing shingles, weak pointing, poor drainage — water will get in. Virtually every water problem starts small, and most can be fixed at very little or no cost if they're noticed — and taken care of — early. But a drop becomes a trickle, then a torrent. What began as a small problem with the flashing or the drainage at the foundation, if left unattended, will turn into a major repair job. Water intrusion is like a toothache: it doesn't get better on its own. Hoping it will go away isn't the answer. Putting off doing something about it — in other words, deferring maintenance — only allows it to grow into a major problem.

Whatever the problem is, get it while it's small.

Make Plans in an Orderly Way

It's easier to get people to give or to pay attention to building improvements that can be seen. However, it's often the case that something that can't be seen needs to be done first. The property support committee that oversees the grant and loan program for the congregations of our diocese has occasionally angered congregational leaders by refusing to approve money for interior cosmetic work when there are exterior jobs that need to be done first. What's the point of fixing the plaster and painting if the roof still leaks? There's no future in treating the symptom and ignoring the disease.

The idea of going about the work your buildings need in an orderly way may also require a big attitude adjustment on the part of your leadership. Congregations frequently benefit tremendously from the volunteer efforts of members and friends who have skills in the building trades. However, these efforts can sometimes be misguided, scattered, and not appropriate. Whether your buildings are new or old, large or small, architecturally significant or humbly plain, your stewardship of the buildings will benefit from having some kind of capital plan.

Don't just do the next thing someone suggests. Make priorities. Maybe your buildings are relatively new and in good condition. You will still benefit from a conditions survey that will estimate the length of the remaining useful lives of major components. If your buildings are older and you know there are many things that need to be done, then you really need the conditions survey to help you set your priorities.

Please spend the money necessary to have the conditions survey done by a qualified professional. The "qualified" part is very important. If you have an old building, you need someone with lots of experience with old buildings. The construction methods and materials used a century ago differ markedly from those used today. You need someone who is qualified to survey your particular buildings and make recommendations appropriate to the building. Some of your fellow leaders may object to what they see as a useless expenditure. "*We* know what needs to be done," they may say. Well, they certainly know *some* of the things that need to be done, but they may not know how to do them *right,* and there are probably others of which no one is aware, and you will probably not be able to prioritize the work and estimate its cost without the help of a qualified professional. It is *not* a waste of money to pay for the professional services you need in order to do things in the best order and in the most appropriate way. You're far more likely to waste money if you start doing things without a plan. A parish in our diocese restored its stunning interior some years ago at significant cost. Unfortunately, the roof should have been done first, as soon became apparent. By the time the roof was replaced, the interior had to be completely restored again. It is even more breathtaking now, but the first restoration turned out to be a waste of a considerable amount of money.

Pay for the professional services required to get a prioritized plan so you can approach your building projects in an orderly way.

Do It Right

Many of our buildings date from the pre-income-tax era. The assumption seems to have been that congregations did not need endowments because there would always be prominent vestrymen (and they *were* men) who could make up the deficit at year's end and fund other needs along the way.

No congregation of my acquaintance can still do business that way. One result has been a great increase in repairs done on the cheap that are incongruent with the rest of the structure. Often these modifications date to the mid-twentieth century before there was a general awareness of the importance of the preservation of historic buildings.

So we have asphalt roofs that replaced slate roofs. We have fake paneling and dropped ceilings in once-grand rooms. We have sheet linoleum over hardwood floors. I suggest that there are two problems with the "let's do the cheapest thing" approach to building maintenance.

The first problem is what it says about our attitude to the legacy of past generations and our lack of faith in the future. What did the one talent in the parable look like after it had been buried all those years by the servant paralyzed by anxiety? If that talent had been a historic church building, the equivalent of burying it might be covering it with aluminum siding on the exterior and particle-board paneling within.

If we believe our congregations have a future, then we want to pass on to our heirs a patrimony at least equivalent to what we received. If, on the other hand, you think you're going out of business, then I suppose it doesn't matter how you limp along until the day you close. The first problem with doing the cheapest thing is that the result silently but insistently proclaims, "You don't want to be part of us. We lack leadership and vision."

The second problem is much more practical: you get what you pay for. I have learned this lesson personally in the decades I've owned nineteenth-century houses. What we did right is still in good shape. Where we "cheaped out" it has cost us more in the long run because we've had to do it again. An asphalt roof costs less up front than a

slate roof, but a proper slate roof properly done lasts a century; a
shingle roof would need to be replaced twice in that time period.

If you don't take the long view, this second point may not be clear.
Yes, it's quite true that an asphalt shingle roof costs less today than
a slate roof. And if we knew that the church had to plan only for
the next thirty or forty years, it would make sense not to plan for
a longer horizon. However, in many cases the buildings we are discussing have already served the congregation for 125 or 150 years.
It is our responsibility in our generation to plan for the next 150
years. Therefore, the slate roof is more economical, not because it
will cost our generation less, but over the next century it costs the
congregation less.

There's another aspect to doing it right. It may seem like a matter
of taste, but I think it goes beyond mere aesthetic preference. Rather,
I see it as related to the Incarnation. Buildings are physical expres-
sions of the age in which they were built. Perhaps the quintessential
"church" styles in this country until recent years were the neo-
classical (think frame New England meetinghouse) and the Gothic
(spires, pointed arch windows, etc.). The Gothic style of church ar-
chitecture started to appear in the 1830s, and for nearly 150 years
most churches were built in different versions of the Gothic style. The
materials and methods used in the 1840s were quite different from
those used in the 1920s, even though the buildings share the same architectural inspiration. Even to the untrained eye there is something
immensely satisfying about a building that has been maintained and
upgraded over the years in a way that is appropriate to the style in
which it was constructed. And even the untrained eye is also unsettled
by needless and sometimes glaring incongruities.

Appropriateness doesn't mean preserving a building in amber. It
was a good thing to retrofit mid-nineteenth-century buildings with
central heating and electrical and plumbing systems. Churches today
should be air-conditioned and accessible to those with disabilities.

The lighting in many churches needs to be updated and improved. And many sound systems I've encountered should be removed and redone. All these things can be done in ways that enhance the impact of the space on those who enter; they can also be done in ways that diminish the experience of being in the building. Don't do things that clash with the architectural integrity of the building. And yes, you need to *pay for* the professional counsel of those who are experienced with these matters and who can suggest and design things that are appropriate for your space. It's worth it. One reason your sound system may be so bad is that it was designed and installed by well-meaning and devoted volunteers. Maybe it's time to call in a sound system engineer.

Do it right. It says that you're grateful for the past and that you have faith in the future. It's less expensive in the long run. And it also keeps worshipers from being distracted by physical discomfort, inadequate lighting, and bad sound.

Reserve for Capital Needs

We've spoken about the need for capital reserves. You simply can't do what needs to be done with your buildings unless you are putting aside funds every year to pay for it. How much do you need to be reserving? There are three ways I know of to calculate what you should be putting aside for capital maintenance and replacement.

Figuring depreciation

Everyone understands the basic concept of depreciation. As soon as you drive a new car off the sales lot, it's worth less because now it's a used car. Figuring depreciation is simply calculating *how much less* something is worth every year as it ages and wears out. And the purpose of figuring *how much less* something is worth is so you know *how much to set aside* to maintain the total value of your assets.

If you replace the old heating system with a $50,000 boiler that has an estimated life of twenty-five years, it is depreciating at $2,000 per year. That's the amount you need to be reserving at interest every year so that in twenty-five years you have $50,000 plus the interest the money has earned to make up for inflation. Assuming a 3 percent inflation rate, it will cost $104,700 in 2025 to replace a $50,000 boiler purchased in 2000. And as we've noted, you need to maintain the system regularly so that it lasts as long as it is supposed to.

Here's how figuring depreciation and putting in reserve the cash equivalent of the depreciation helps you maintain the total value of your assets. When you take some of the $250,000 in cash that you have and put on a new roof for $100,000, you haven't actually decreased your assets. Instead of $250,000 in cash assets, you now have $150,000 in cash and a new roof worth $100,000. Even though your disbursed the cash to pay for the roof, it wasn't an expense that shows up on your statement of revenue and expenses. It stays on the balance sheet (the listing of assets and liabilities) because you've transferred the $100,000 from a current asset (cash) to a depreciable asset (the roof).

Before you replace the roof

Cash	$250,000
Total assets	$250,000

After you replace the roof

Cash	$150,000
Cost of roof	100,000
Total assets	$250,000

The expense shows up over the forty years the roof is supposed to last. Every year the roof is worth $2,500 less ($100,000/forty years). The value of the fixed asset is reduced every year by $2,500 in depreciation. The $2,500 depreciation shows up as an expense every year in your statement of revenue and expenses. It is a noncash expense because you laid out the cash when you bought the roof, but it's still a real reduction in your assets. It represents *how much less* your total assets are worth every year as the roof gets older. After ten years, assuming nothing else changed with your cash, you'd have cash of $150,000, but the roof would be worth only $75,000. Your total assets are down $25,000 because of the depreciation on the roof.

After ten years with no capital reserve	
Cash	$150,000
Cost of roof	100,000
(Less accumulated depreciation)	(25,000)
Total assets	$225,000

Putting the amount equal to the depreciation expense every year into a capital reserve account preserves the value of your total assets. If every year you put $2,500 into your reserve account as you charged the $2,500 depreciation expense, at the end of ten years, assuming no other changes in your cash, the roof would be worth $75,000, but you would have $175,000 in cash, the $150,000 you had plus the $25,000 you had reserved over the ten-year period. You've preserved the value of your total assets, and, of course, you also have the interest the capital reserve fund has earned over the years.

After ten years with a capital reserve	
Cash	$150,000
Capital reserve for roof	25,000
Cost of roof	100,000
(Less accumulated depreciation)	(25,000)
Total assets	$250,000

In order to be able to put aside the $2,500 every year, you need to receive in income $2,500 more than you lay out in cash expenses. That gives you the extra $2,500 to put aside into the capital reserve account. If you capitalize fixed assets and post the depreciation expense every year, and if adding the depreciation expense throws your revenue and expense statement into deficit, it means that you don't have the cash to set aside in the capital reserve fund. I've heard people say, "We don't really have a deficit because it's only the depreciation that put us in the red, and that's not a cash expense." They're a little bit right, but mostly wrong. Depreciation is indeed a noncash expense, but it is a real expense nonetheless. If you can't set aside the amount of depreciation every year in the capital reserve account, you are operating at a deficit. And that deficit will come back to bite the congregation at some point when the roof wears out and there's no money to replace it. You may be gone by then, but those who have to pick up the pieces will have cause to remember you. Make sure they remember you as the generation that got it right.

Although in theory figuring depreciation will give you the most accurate way of determining how much you need to be reserving every year, there are some significant practical drawbacks to this approach.

First, many churches are on the cash basis of accounting and do not capitalize fixed assets. If you're on the cash basis, you show the full cost of the capital improvement in the year that you've spent the money, instead of reducing your assets year by year by the amount of depreciation.

Second, even those churches that are on the accrual basis of accounting and do capitalize fixed assets and calculate depreciation have probably come to that system only recently as more and more churches present their financial statements in accordance with generally accepted auditing standards. The amounts entered for fixed assets and depreciation may be estimates that satisfy the accountants but do not give an accurate idea of the actual wear and tear on existing systems and components.

Finally, figuring with any accuracy the annual depreciation of your fixed assets is pretty tedious. There are lots of schedules and lots of entries. Probably only the largest churches have the professional finance staff needed to maintain the system, and the inherent fussiness of what is required to maintain it tends to make people impatient, as does the extra money the annual audit costs if you have the auditors maintain the depreciation schedules. A volunteer treasurer who is able to do it will likely be succeeded by a treasurer who can't. (If volunteers keep your books, it's better to have a simple system that your successors can keep up than an accurate, but complex, system that a less proficient successor might not be able to maintain.)

In short, as a practical matter, chances are good that you don't have a way of figuring depreciation. As long as you understand the concept and realize that you have to be setting something aside, don't despair; there are two other ways to come up with a number.

Replacement insurance cost

A way to get a (very rough) idea of what you should be setting aside in a capital reserve fund is to look at your insurance policy. If you have replacement value insurance, and I hope you do, the insured value of the buildings is the insurance carrier's estimate of what it would cost to rebuild your plant in the event of a total loss.

Let me make a small digression here about insurance. If you don't have replacement value insurance, you probably are insured for "actual value," which means cost less depreciation. Although the annual premiums are cheaper for this kind of insurance, in the event of a loss, the settlement you would receive would almost certainly not be sufficient to make the repairs. Especially in congregations with large historic plants, I've heard leaders say, "If this building is destroyed, we certainly won't rebuild anything like this." That may be true, but you're more likely to have a partial loss than a total loss. If a fire damages part of the church, you'll want to be able to restore it so it matches the part that was not damaged, and you won't be able to do that without replacement value insurance. In the event of a total loss, you probably won't be able to rebuild much of anything unless you have replacement value insurance. Please make sure your insurance coverage is adequate.

If you assume that the estimate for the cost of replacement is accurate and that components and systems will need to be replaced on a forty-year cycle, you can aim to set aside 2.5 percent of the replacement cost every year in the capital reserve fund. You might want to be sitting down when you make this calculation. If your buildings are insured for $2 million, the forty-year rule of thumb means that you should be setting aside $50,000 every year in the capital reserve account. If my experience is any guide, whatever the 2.5 percent works out to be is likely to seem an astronomical sum. You may need to sit there for a few minutes in stunned silence.

When you've regained the power of speech, don't say, "This is impossible. We can't do that." There's one more way to make some headway.

Take some disciplined steps

At least now you have an idea of what you should be setting aside, based on either depreciation or the insurance value. You may not be reserving anything right now. The gap between what is and what ought to be may seem unbridgeable. Here's a way to start across the chasm.

Transfer the "Major Repairs" budget line to a reserve fund. You probably have some kind of budget line for "Maintenance and Repairs" and some kind of line for "Major Repairs." The first one is probably for cleaning supplies, light bulbs, contracts for snow removal or lawn care, and so on. You know what it costs you for basic maintenance to keep the buildings open. The "Major Repairs" line is something you have in the budget because you know that things can go wrong that absolutely need to be fixed: the boiler breaks down, the refrigerator conks out, or there's a leak in the plumbing. So you put a line in the budget, and then you try to get through the year without spending it. If you're able to reach December 31 without having to spend much of it, you breathe a sigh of relief and try to get through the next year without spending any of the line. Maybe you even reduce the line in the next year's budget because apparently you don't need it. Of course, you know you're borrowing from the future. You know that something will happen someday, and you'll have to come up with the money to fix it.

The first tiny step you can take toward reserving appropriately for capital needs is to *transfer* the full amount of that budget line out of your checking account into some separate interest-bearing money market account, CD, or savings account. The line in your operating budget will be fully "expended" every year because you will have transferred the funds from the operating account to the capital reserve account. Then you make major repairs from what you've transferred.

Increase the transfer every year. The second step is to increase that line a little every year and to make sure that you transfer the full amount out of the operating fund to reduce the temptation to spend it on other operating expenses. Commit yourselves to increasing this figure, and make sure you increase it every year. If you're not reserving adequately for capital needs, you are running up the institutional equivalent of credit card debt. Don't be anxious about it; just resolve that the practice won't continue, and exercise the leadership necessary to see that the practice doesn't continue. Make sure that there's a substantial increase in what you put away every year.

Direct a recurring income stream into the reserve. Another idea is to put some regular recurring income stream directly into the capital reserve account without letting it go through the operating budget. Possible sources for this income stream include all or part of the drawdown from your long-term investments, the net proceeds of a regular fund-raising event or events, or the net income from some property rental.

Maybe you think it's not possible to divert one of these other income streams to the capital reserve fund because they're all needed for the operating budget. If funds are needed for the capital reserve account, maybe you think the way to get them is to appeal to the congregation. I do not recommend funding the capital reserve by asking the congregation for special gifts. As you'll see in chapter 6, I believe that in a financially and programmatically healthy congregation about three-fourths or more of the operating budget comes from the membership. However, I don't think you get there with a congregational culture that favors small pledges and lots of special appeals. I suggest working to change the culture of your congregation so that people make a substantial pledge of a percentage of their income toward the operating expenses of the congregation. Then don't nickel-and-dime them.

Besides, you need to come up with the funds for the capital reserve year after year, and special appeals don't work over time. If such appeals are the norm, then they're not special any longer. In the wake of some crisis, people will often respond generously. After a year or two, contributions will dwindle, and you'll be back at square one.

Identify some projects to keep your focus. If you've done the conditions survey we spoke of earlier, there are sure to be two or three critical items (roof, heating plant, painting) that should be seen to over the next five to ten years. Decide that the bulk of what you are reserving will go toward these projects. You won't be able to save all of the reserve for these items, because other things will probably need attention along the way. However, devoting three-fourths of the reserve to these projects will keep you from frittering the money away on small cosmetic projects that you probably could easily raise additional funds for. These projects will likely be the less "sexy" ones that are vital for the integrity of the building but are harder to raise money for.

The goal is to work toward a way to fund the capital reserve, either through a line in the operating budget or by directing some regular recurring income stream into the capital reserve. To keep your focus, identify several important capital projects that you know will be coming up over the next ten years, and work toward funding them through the reserve. Even though the gap may seem enormous when you start, here as elsewhere, I think you will discover that if you develop a vision, and outline an orderly plan for implementing the vision, your members will respond. People tend to come on board when the ship is heading somewhere they want to go and when those responsible have demonstrated that they know how to sail it.

Keep Records

This may seem unimportant, but for building systems it's crucial. When our property support director visits a parish and asks how old the roof is, or when the boiler was installed, in an amazing number of instances no one knows and there are no records anywhere. Documents about major capital projects should be kept permanently. I am aware that good files are often a casualty of the press of events. Usually the minutes of the governing board are preserved, however, even if other papers that should be in the permanent file may not be. Please at least ensure that important acts are fully recorded in the minutes. It's a good idea to list these significant decisions in the reports to the annual meeting. Remember the future when you're preparing these documents. Those minutes and reports are the primary historical documents of your congregation, and even if no one ever writes a detailed history of your parish, please remember that in twenty years people will need to know how old the furnace is or when the windows were restored.

Call on Assistance

This topic comes at the end of the chapter not because it's least important, but so that you'll remember it. It's the *most* important point. Please don't try to do this all on your own. You'll do a better job if you call in others to help. Your diocese, synod, presbytery, or conference may have both financial and technical resources available to you. If your judicatory doesn't, there will probably be resources at the national level of your denomination. And please *pay for* the professional help you need. You'll have better results. You'll probably also save money by doing first things first and by doing all things in the most appropriate way.

If your building is architecturally significant or of historic interest, other resources are available the might be able to assist you. Refer to the Web site that accompanies this book (*www.churchpublishing.org/ rememberthefuture)* for a few national and regional organizations that help congregations with historic buildings.

Chapter 5

Outside Use of Your Buildings

So be wise as serpents and innocent as doves.
— Matthew 10:16b

For which of you, intending to build a tower, does not first sit down and estimate the cost, to see whether he has enough to complete it?
— Luke 14:28

Many congregations have buildings in addition to the church and the parsonage or rectory. From the mid-nineteenth century onward, many churches built parish houses with substantial facilities — auditoriums, gymnasiums, kitchens, meeting rooms, even bowling alleys. These "institutional parishes" did community outreach to young people and the needy at a time when both extracurricular activities at schools and government-funded social services were unknown.

Since these facilities were intended to serve needs beyond worship and Christian education, it is not unusual for congregations to have space beyond what they need for their liturgical, educational, and social life. A century ago the underserved population was young people, and although there are still tremendous opportunities for programs for young people, the people you're likely to be serving now include the elderly, preschoolers, the homeless, and the hungry.

Most congregations are generous about letting groups have weekly or monthly meetings. AARP chapters, 12-step groups of all kinds, civic associations, and all kinds of other groups meet regularly in

115

church halls. Very often little more here is required than a mutual understanding of the rate they'll pay, setup, cleanup, and some rules posted about the kitchen, the lights, and opening and closing. It's a very good idea to have these matters set down in writing so there won't be any confusion, but there usually isn't very much confusion about the arrangements for these meetings, unless there's a change in leadership in the group that's having the meetings. As long as the same individuals are in charge of the meetings, there won't be much that goes wrong, and, if there is, a phone call usually can set it right.

I strongly recommend a memorandum of understanding with anybody who uses your space even for monthly meetings, but the focus of this chapter is not on your arrangements with groups that use your space just for meetings. The focus here is on your relationships with any groups that use your space to provide their services; this includes everything from ballet lessons and nursery schools to community theater programs to feeding programs and homeless shelters.

Congregations often derive income by permitting outside groups to use their extra space. However, not all arrangements between congregations and outside groups have been happy and harmonious. In this chapter we discuss lessons that some congregations have learned through difficult experiences. Most of the difficulties have come from not thinking things through at the outset and, of course, by failing to remember the future.

In order to think through exactly what you're trying to accomplish when letting others use your space, I think you need to ask some questions.

Why Are You Letting Outside Groups Use Your Space?

Are you doing this because you think it will attract members? Be very careful, and read the following sections. If you're thinking of renting your space to an outside program because you think it will attract members, I'm sorry to tell you that you'll probably be disappointed.

Are you doing this to make money? That's fine. Be clear about how much you want to make, the need to reserve funds for capital maintenance, and possible tax implications.

Are you doing it as part of your outreach? That's fine. Be clear about what it's going to cost you, whether you can afford it, and whether this is where you'd like to direct those resources.

Do you think you're doing it for a combination of these? It is possible at times to do well by doing good, but you need to consider carefully the various aspects of what you are envisioning. It happens all too frequently, as we will see, that when you're trying to accomplish two or more objectives, you end up accomplishing none.

Get clear and stay clear on what you are trying to do. Think through the implications and the direct and indirect costs of your plans.

"We'll Get People to Join Our Congregation"

It is a good thing for your buildings to be used. If you have the space, it is a good thing to open the doors wide and let your spaces be used for community functions and community programs. If you have the space available, it is not at all a bad thing to make some money toward the costs of operating your buildings by renting out spaces when you're not using them. It is very unlikely, however, that your congregation will grow as a result of any outside group's use of your space.

The parents of the children in the nursery school that meets in your parish house may love the school and be grateful for a good program in a safe space. Very few of them will become members of your congregation because of the nursery school. People may love the concert series that local musicians run, and they may flock to the productions of the community theater company that performs in your auditorium. Almost none of them will be in your pews on Sunday morning as a result of those programs. You may receive recognition and awards because of the feeding programs and after-school tutoring programs that operate on your site. A few people may join your congregation because of its commitment to community service, but chances are there won't be very many of them.

In my observation and experience, you don't build a congregation by simply allowing others to conduct their programs in your buildings. If people are going to join you on Sunday mornings, it'll be because they find something compelling going on at those Sunday services, not because they find worthwhile programs operating on your site the other six and a half days, and especially not because other people are operating worthwhile programs using your spaces.

Such programs don't build the congregation; it happens the other way around. The love and concern of a vital congregation find expression in programs that minister to human need. When a program grows out of the desire of the congregation to meet a community need, that program may well contribute to the growth of the congregation. Such programs will certainly contribute to the spiritual growth of your members on whose volunteer labor they depend. The congregation will not grow, however, just because you're letting a counseling center or a school or a theater company rent your space.

"It's Part of Our Outreach"

Very often congregations explain to themselves that they're not concerned with what they're getting from an outside group because "it's part of our outreach." The approach may be valid if it's really true and if you have thought through all of its implications.

There are at least three questions to ask. First, is it really our outreach? Second, if it is our outreach, can we afford it? Third, are we expecting others to subsidize us?

The first question is really two questions. First, is it outreach? Second, is it *our* outreach? I can't answer these questions since I don't know your circumstances, but I can tell you that I've seen a number of unfocused and even self-serving ways people have answered these questions. Take theater companies, for instance. Whether you mount theatrical productions as a parish-sponsored activity or allow a community theater group to use your space, it might be a lot of fun for those involved and it may be a great thing in the community, but it probably isn't outreach. It's fair to ask whether such a program should be directly or indirectly subsidized by the parish budget. (And permit me to observe that theater productions are such an all-consuming enterprise involving a fair amount of gear and mess that you want to think very, very clearly about hosting a theater company unless you can provide space dedicated to their work. Despite all kinds of good intentions, it's very hard for theatrical companies to share space when they're in the throes of rehearsal, set construction, and production. Let those who have ears to hear learn from the difficult experiences of others.)

The second part of the question is also worth asking: it is *our* outreach? This builds on the discussion in the previous section. Is this something you're doing, or it is something others are doing using your space? Please be as clear as you can about this self-examination. It matters. If it's really someone else's outreach, it's perfectly all right to let it happen in your space, but you'll be more of a landlord than a participant. You may decide to be a landlord that loses money on the deal, but you should decide that up front.

If the tenant is using the buildings at times when the congregation doesn't use them, it means significantly higher costs for utilities. If the tenant is paying less than the cost of the additional heat and electricity, is that something the parish budget can afford? Don't let the outside organization or some of your leaders guilt you into doing something that you don't have the will or the money to do. Don't end up subsidizing the operation in a way that your finances can't really permit.

Please be clear about the costs and who is expected to pay them. Some of our congregations that are renting out most of a parish house to an outside group have applied to our diocesan property support committee for a grant for a new roof for the building. When asked why they have not reserved funds for the capital maintenance of an income-producing property, the congregations have responded, "It's part of our outreach." The property support committee has often decided that it is unfair for a congregation to ask the entire diocese for an indirect subsidy of its "outreach" programs, particularly since the congregations hadn't thought to include a reserve for capital maintenance in the arrangement.

Mixed Motives Can Make a Mess

Here's a situation I've encountered in more than one congregation. The bottom floor of what used to be the rectory is used for meeting rooms; the upper floor makes an apartment for a sexton. There's a vague (and always unwritten) understanding that the sexton will do certain jobs around the church in exchange for free or a much-reduced rent. The vestry tells itself (and me, when I ask) that "this is part of our outreach" because the sexton has a history of some personal problems.

In other words, the parish is taking a loss on the operating expenses of the apartment and is receiving nothing to set aside into a capital reserve account to keep the former parsonage in good repair. In addition, the leaders and parishioners are naturally dissatisfied with the sexton's performance. How could it be otherwise, when there is no job description and the duties are undefined? In addition, the sexton feels alternately self-conscious because she knows she isn't really earning the break she's getting in the rent, and offended because some parishioners are less than nice to her about the situation. The sexton also resents that the parish, given the situation, is not too careful about the upkeep of the apartment.

So the full costs of this kind of "outreach" are a good bit higher than they appear, both financially and with regard to interpersonal relationships. The arrangement is failing to accomplish any of the goals people had when they set it up. The work isn't getting done, the apartment is losing money, and the caretaker doesn't have a really adequate place to live. Besides, nobody has thought about the tax implications of the arrangement. In most states a house comes off the property tax rolls if it is used for housing the cleric serving the congregation that owns it. If it's used as a rental property, the congregation probably owes property tax on it. In addition, when any employer, churches included, provides housing to a lay employee, in almost every case the value of the housing is fully subject to Social Security and Medicare tax, plus federal, state, and local income taxes. If you're knocking $600 a month off the fair market rent in exchange for the services to be provided, then the taxable income resulting from the arrangement is $7,200 annually.

Clearly thought out expectations and clearly articulated arrangements would serve everyone better. Get rent for the apartment that at least allows you to keep it in good repair. Draw up a job description for the sexton with clear duties and lines of supervision, and pay an appropriate compensation for the sexton from the proceeds of the rental. (And have the payroll processed professionally: everyone will sleep better at night.)

If you want to do outreach, first figure out whether it's really your outreach and what all the costs are, and then figure out if you are able and willing to pay them.

What Can You Afford to Let Others Use?

Some congregations, caught in a budget crunch, have allowed outside groups to use so much space that there is not enough room left for parish life to go on. It's difficult to have a warm and welcoming coffee hour when the parish hall is set up for a nursery school and you have to have fellowship in tiny chairs or out in the hall.

Do not let yourselves feel compelled to cede space that you need to function as a congregation. To cripple your parish life for a short-term budget fix is contrary to the long-term vision I have been urging. Before you arrange to let a group use your space, make sure that you can afford to give up the space. If the space is to be shared, it is crucially important to define the arrangements carefully and thoroughly.

How Much Should They Pay?

There are three ways to get an answer, and you need to look at *all three* before you settle with the outside group.

1. What does similar space cost in your area?

You may not be a commercial landlord, but you need to know what the rents for similar spaces and similar uses are in your neighborhood. Real estate is always local; vague anecdotes about costs in other times and places just won't do. You have to do some real checking with real estate agents in your area.

Rental prices are always given in terms of so many dollars per square foot. To translate this into your context, you have to know how many square feet you are thinking of letting the outside group use. It is stupefying, but one finds over and over that a congregation has signed an agreement with a space user without knowing how many square feet they are letting the group use. Measure the space.

Calculate the number of square feet. Find out what similar space is renting for in your area.

2. *What does it cost us to run the space?*

In order to know whether the money you receive from the outside user is a fair amount, you have to know what it will cost you to offer the space. You know what it costs overall to operate your buildings every year. The amounts for property and casualty insurance, utilities, maintenance supplies and repairs, janitorial services, and so on, are in your operating budget. However, you can't tell from the total annual costs how much it costs you to let an outside group use the parish hall four evenings a week at times it's not being used now. You need to find out how much it costs to operate your space per square foot and per hour.

You can download a sample of the worksheet I'm about to describe from the Web site that accompanies this book (*www.churchpublishing .org/rememberthefuture*). You'll have to enter your own numbers, but the formulas are already there.

You measure the various spaces in your buildings and calculate the square feet in each space. Then you figure out how many hours per week and how many weeks per year each space is used. By multiplying the square feet of each space by the total number of hours per year the space is used, you find out how many "square-foot hours" of active use your spaces have.

Then you add up the overhead costs of running your buildings, including insurance, utilities, janitorial services, supplies, repairs, and the funding of your capital reserve. You'll come to a dollar total. Divide that total by the total number of square-foot hours, and you'll find out how much it costs you to operate one square foot of your space for one hour.

Because the worksheet is based on your current usage, you can get an idea of what it costs you now to run your space. Be sure to include in the calculation the amount you are setting aside every year into your capital reserve fund. The cost of providing the space includes not only oil, utilities, insurance, janitorial services, and supplies; it includes also the funds you set aside to do capital improvements and capital maintenance.

Remember as well that if you are negotiating with a nursery school or a social service agency that will use your facilities all week long during times when the space is not now being used, you will have to take into the account the added cost of heat and electricity. Remember, they'll want air conditioners in the summer. (Your parishioners probably want air conditioning as well, but that's another discussion!)

Utilities aren't the only operating costs that might go up when you rent. There will probably be higher costs for maintenance supplies, water and sewage charges, and garbage pickup, if you have to pay for that. Depending on the kind of tenant, perhaps the workload on your parish administrator or sexton will increase, and you'll have higher personnel costs. Think this one out carefully and all the way through.

Only when you know the answers to both questions 1 and 2 should you discuss the following:

3. What can the group afford to pay?

Too often this is the only question congregations ask, with the result that the space is rented for far below what it is worth and even below what it costs to provide the space. Congregations sometimes actually lose money on space rentals when they had intended to get some help with the budget.

The right answer to the question of the right rent will be a combination of the answers you get to all three of these ways of calculating the fair price. You cannot hope to get to the right answer unless you (a) measure your space, (b) find out what similar space goes for in your area, and (c) figure what it will cost you to provide that amount of space for the number of hours per week the group will be using it.

Get It Clear and in Writing

I have ceased being surprised that congregations do not have any written agreements with the organizations that use their space.

I have never been surprised that congregations with no clear written agreements with outside users usually have conflicts and problems with the users.

It is neither fussy nor malicious to take the time to work out the specifics of a group's use of space and to reduce it to writing. A clear oral understanding reached in January will by October be hazy and remembered differently by various parties. The individuals on both sides who came to the "clear" oral understanding will pass from the scene. Their successors will be left with misunderstandings and conflicts.

Get it in writing, and make sure there are provisions for regular communication and review.

The Owner Proposes the Lease

If you owned a two-family house and were renting the apartment, you probably wouldn't ask the prospective tenant to draft the lease. Yet very often congregations that lack access to legal expertise ask the outside user to propose the terms for using their space. If you do it that way, don't be surprised if the outside organization pays more attention to its interests than to yours.

Many judicatories have devised model leases that congregations can adapt to their specific circumstances. Check with your judicatory, or download the model lease from the Web site of a judicatory that has one. There are some samples on the Web site accompanying this book (*www.churchpublishing.org/rememberthefuture*).

I encourage you not to be penny-wise and pound-foolish. If you are entering a complicated and long-term arrangement with a prospective tenant, pay for legal counsel to make sure your interests are protected. It is foolish to "save" the several hundred dollars a lawyer's services might cost and then live for years with the consequences of a poorly devised lease. Here as elsewhere, I strongly encourage you to *pay for* the professional services you need. You cannot do a good job of managing the assets in your care without the appropriate services of professionals.

And be willing to pay for those services so you can insist on getting good service. If someone is willing to do it *pro bono,* that's fine, but don't be a beggar about it. Local physicians offered my father, a poorly paid American Baptist minister, "professional courtesy" services in the days when doctors made house calls. My father insisted on paying so that, as he said, "They'll come when I call."

Insurance Matters

The basic insurance you have on your building is called property and casualty insurance. That policy covers not only damage to your property from fire and other calamities, but it also indemnifies your liability in case someone is injured on your property. Common liability claims arise from "slip and fall" cases, when someone sues you alleging injury from falling on your sidewalk because the walk was not properly maintained. Your property and casualty insurance defends you in such cases. Your insurance policy also normally covers all parish-sponsored activities, whether they take place on your property or off-site. You need to keep your insurance carrier up to date with all your activities so you can be sure you are covered.

When outside groups hold activities on your site, those activities also need to be insured. Sometimes regular meetings of outside groups are properly covered by your insurance. For example, 12-step groups typically do not have their own insurance, and you can normally consider their meetings parish-sponsored activities, as long as you have properly informed your carrier and conform to the requirements of your policy.

In other cases the outside groups using your space should provide you with evidence that they are insured and that their activities on your site are covered by their insurance. This evidence is normally in the form of a Certificate of Insurance. The certificate is issued by the outside group's insurance carrier. It should name you as an additional insured. The certificate lists the kinds of coverage involved and the period covered.

When individuals use your space for a birthday party or other celebration, very often their homeowner's insurance can provide coverage for the event. If you are making a long-term arrangement with an outside agency that will provide programs on your site, the lease should require the tenant to provide every year a current Certificate of Insurance during the term of the lease.

If organizations or contractors will be having their own employees working on your property, you want to make sure that those employees are covered for workers' compensation insurance. All people working for pay on your site need to be covered by workers' comp. If a person employed by someone else is injured while working on your property, and if it turns out that the person's employer was not providing coverage, you will be liable. There can be additional complications in some states that you'll want to check out with your insurance carrier. You want to take the time to make sure that anyone else's employees working on your property are covered by workers' compensation insurance if it is required in your state.

Look Down the Road and around the Corners

The agreement with outside entities using your facilities should not only state the current understanding. It should consider contingencies that might develop. It's crucial to remember the future at this point. These are not just the picky concerns of lawyers and accountants. Jesus counseled us to be "wise as serpents and innocent as doves" (Matt. 10:16), and he cautioned us, before embarking on a project, to "sit down first and estimate the cost" (Luke 14:28). Innocence without wisdom and actions without foresight are not virtuous.

What about Taxes?

Renting your space never jeopardizes your status as a tax-exempt charitable organization. However, renting space may have tax implications. By the way, you won't avoid these implications by calling the rent you charge a "donation." Governmental agencies have better definitions than we sometimes do. If you receive something in return for your money, like the use of your facility, the money is not a gift; it's a payment. So if it's rent, call it rent. It'll help you define what a real donation is.

First, if there is a mortgage on the property, rental income will probably be subject to federal Unrelated Business Income Tax (UBIT). Income from renting parking spaces is normally subject to this tax. The purpose of UBIT is to eliminate the unfair competitive advantage that not-for-profits would enjoy if they could sell products or provide services to the public in direct competition with taxable enterprises. However, most of the time, the income you derive from those using your space is not subject to UBIT. In other words, with exceptions such as those noted above, you are not subject to any kind of income tax on the revenue you receive from space rentals.

Second, there are circumstances under which leasing space to out-side groups, including other not-for-profits, can result in the leased property being put back on the local property tax rolls. For example, in most states the house a congregation provides for its cleric is excluded from property tax. Normally you lose the property tax exemption if you rent the house to someone else or allow a lay employee to live in it. The house can come off the property tax rolls again when it is occupied by your cleric.

That there may be tax implications doesn't mean it is a bad idea to rent the property. It just means that the UBIT or property taxes may be some of the costs you have to figure into the deal. One suggestion is to have the tenant reimburse the property owner for the property taxes separately from the rent. Or you can do what commercial land-lords do: calculate the taxes into the rent per square foot. The taxes are just part of your overhead.

A lot of people who pay corporate income tax and property taxes make money on real estate rentals. Congregations can as well. You just need to plan well and consider all aspects of the deal.

Do We Have to Get Approval?

If you are an Episcopal congregation, you need the approvals of the diocesan bishop and standing committee if the term of the lease is for five years or more. That includes leases whose initial term is shorter than five years but which give the tenant the right to renew so that the lease could extend for more than five years. Some other denominations have their own requirements for ecclesiastical consents. The necessary approvals might also involve the civil authorities. In New York State, for example, all not-for-profit corporations, including all religious corporations, need the approval of the court of the county in which they are incorporated to mortgage or sell real property, or to lease property for five years or more.

The purpose of these consents is not to make life difficult. The purpose is to provide a third-party review of the arrangement you contemplate entering to make sure that it is in the long-term best interest of the congregation. Too often the ecclesiastical consent process simply checks the paperwork and rubber stamps the congregation's decision, but in my opinion the reviews at this level should be substantive. If approvals are required, the congregation should be in touch with the diocese or judicatory as soon as any deal begins to take shape, so that a congregation doesn't present the body whose approval is required with a fait accompli.

If you need the consent of your judicatory, greet this requirement as an opportunity to be accountable to the larger church for your stewardship of your congregation's assets. Be sure that you've done your homework so that you can demonstrate that you have considered the economic and programmatic consequences of the transaction.

If you don't need the approval of anyone outside your congregation, I'm sorry to hear it. Structures of accountability don't always succeed in holding people accountable, but people are more likely to feel accountable when they're part of a structure that could review their actions. I would suggest, difficult as it may be, that you act as if the deal you put together were going to be subject to the review of a disinterested third party.

Get the Assistance You Need

As always, you are not alone. This may be the first time your congregation is entering into a lease. There are plenty of people out there with experience who can help you avoid trouble. Don't think you have to invent the wheel all over again. Check with neighboring congregations. Check with your judicatory. Review the Web site that accompanies this book (*www.churchpublishing.org/rememberthefuture*). The resources are there. Call on them.

Chapter 6

Support from Your Members

And they came, everyone whose heart was stirred, and everyone whose spirit was willing, and brought the Lord's offering to be used for the tent of meeting, and for all its service, and for the sacred vestments. So they came, both men and women; all who were of a willing heart.... —Exodus 34:21–22a

In previous chapters we have looked at land, investments, reserve funds, building upkeep, and considerations about leasing space to outside groups. As you work to marshal the resources necessary to meet today's needs, it is necessary to remember the needs of the future. I've tried to give you ways to consider the long-term implications of the decisions you make today. We church leaders are stewards, not owners. The most important task church leaders have is to prepare for their successors.

The Lure of "Other People's Money"

Most of what we have discussed so far has come from others. Others gave or purchased the land. Others built the buildings. Others bequeathed the endowments. Others are leasing our spaces and paying us rent. In short, probably everything we've talked about so far is what you might call "other people's money."

Other people's money is extremely seductive. I mean, it's tempting to think that other people's money will pay to keep our parish going.

It's tempting to imagine that other people will pay for the handsome building we admire and the warm fellowship we enjoy. It's tempting to think that we should be able to have all that at others' expense without putting much of our own money into it. From what I have seen, many of our congregations have given in to this temptation.

I have met with vestries, finance committees, and budget committees of all sorts and conditions of congregations. When there's a budget problem, it's usually in the line called "Pledge Income," and the problem almost always is that the total plate and pledge is not a big enough percentage of the budgeted expenses.

In most denominations, congregations file with their regional judicatories or national offices an annual report of membership, attendance, stewardship, and finances. In the Episcopal Church the annual filing is commonly called the parochial report. According to the 2003 parochial reports for the Episcopal Diocese of New York, individuals gave about 52 percent of what was needed to pay the regular operating expenses. The median percentage is not dramatically different. In half of our congregations individual giving provides 63 percent or more of operating expenses; in half, individuals provide less than 63 percent of what is needed to run the parish. For the Episcopal Church as a whole in 2003, Plate and Pledge contributions reported covered on average 57 percent of total operating expenses. Averages are usually skewed to some extent by extremes at one end, but it's clear that there are plenty of "normal" congregations where the giving of the current members accounts for less than one-half of the budget.

Averages don't reflect any particular congregation, so in your parish budget the percentage of total operating expenses that is given by your members will likely be different. If you have no endowment and few opportunities for rental income, it is very likely that your people will need to pay 90 percent or more of what the parish operation costs. When the parish has significant endowments or the ability to derive income from rentals, I have seen giving as low as 10 percent of budgeted expenses. By the way, I have seen this 10 percent figure in parishes both large and small. The size and outward success of the parish don't seem to be determinative; what matters is whether the members — whether very few or very many, poor or rich — expect some other source of funds, that is to say, someone else's money, to pay for the operation of their parish.

We are talking about the costs of the current operation, not capital funding. Remember: unless you're funding your capital reserve fund every year from regular sources of income, you still have a budget deficit. You need to find a steady income stream that can be transferred to the capital reserve fund every year. You can't depend on extra contributions from your members for this purpose. If you receive rental or endowment income, I recommend that you work to get to the point where those funds can be put into your capital reserve fund so you can keep up with building needs.

In a financially healthy parish of any size, about three-quarters or more of the operating budget comes from pledges and other gifts from the current members, such as the plate offering, and Christmas and Easter offerings. When more than 20 to 25 percent of the operating budget comes from fund-raising events, space rental, and endowment, I can be pretty confident that the parish is depending too heavily on other people's money. Others who analyze congregations have come to similar conclusions. A senior consultant with the Alban Institute, Dan Hotchkiss, has noted that if the percentage of the operating budget that comes from the membership is less than 80 percent, it would be fair to ask if the congregation feels an appropriate sense of ownership and responsibility. (See the self-survey he has created at *www.alban.org/pdf/CongBudgetSelfTest.pdf.*)

Of course there are exceptions, but in my opinion they are fewer than we might think. Some very large urban congregations with plants of extraordinary size and architectural significance might be able to make the case that the percentage of the budget that comes from the membership can reasonably be lower, given their circumstances. In other circumstances congregations might require long-term assistance from the judicatory. In my experience, however, regardless of the size of your budget, the proportion that currently comes from the membership is likely to be too low.

Bringing It Home, Keeping It Real

So now it's time to bring the discussion home. From here on I'll be talking about *your* money, not about other people's money. That is to say, I plan to talk about the money the current members give to support the work of the congregation, and of course I mean to include the entire leadership, lay and ordained. As leaders of the institution, you are the ones who are most likely involved in asking the rest of the members to give in support of the congregation. It is crucial that you do not ask others to do something that you are not doing, and I say this for two main reasons.

First, the odor of hypocrisy is unmistakable, and where it is present, everyone can smell it, even if they might not be fully conscious of what seems wrong. It is very awkward to listen to a stewardship pitch from a member of the clergy or a lay leader who is suggesting that others do something when it is fairly clear that the person making the pitch is not doing it. Please don't fall through the "hypocrisy crack" that opens up whenever our words are not a sincere expression of our actions. People can tell, and they'll be put off. This is one of the ways in which congregations are different from other organizations. There is a kind of immediate accountability to the membership and to the world that wise leaders come to welcome. Because our faith is precisely that God's grace can transform our lives and convert us, converted and transformed lives are the only effective witness and inspiration.

Second, I firmly believe that we church leaders will make appropriate decisions about the assets that have been left to us by others only if we're putting a substantial amount of our own money into the parish. In my observation and experience, leaders who hope or expect that other people's money will pay for their parish are more likely to sell property unwisely, overspend the endowment, defer maintenance, and rent out space for a quick buck. On the other hand, leaders who are giving back to God a percentage of what God has just given them are less likely to rely too much on other people's money, and they aren't shy about speaking to the rest of the members about the experience of tithing or proportional giving, that is, the practice of giving a percentage off the top of what you just received. It's not surprising to find that visionary leaders of the institution and wise managers of the church's resources are those who are good and faithful stewards of their own funds.

Stewardship and Fund-Raising

Churches appropriately do both stewardship formation and fund-raising, but the two are not the same. Fund-raising is how the leaders of the institution garner support from the membership for the programmatic purposes of the institution. Coming to understand oneself as a steward is a personal transformation that happens in individual members.

Church fund-raising, like any kind of not-for-profit fund-raising, starts from the assumption that people make decisions and choices about how to use their own resources. Given the right kind of preparation and presentation, people can be motivated to direct some of their resources to benefit the church or not-for-profit. Institutions do fund-raising to meet their capital and programmatic needs and goals. The members or supporters of the institution respond because they agree with the mission of the organization and want to help its programs succeed. They are willing, therefore, to take some of their hard-earned money and pay membership dues to public broadcasting stations, buy tickets for a museum's fund-raising dinner, sponsor a child overseas, and make a pledge to their parish church.

Stewardship begins with the insight that everything belongs to God, and that God has entrusted part of the Creation to each of us. We are trustees, fiduciaries, or stewards; we are not owners. When stewards give, they are making a thank-offering to the Giver who has given them all they have. And while the rest that stewards keep is certainly under their control, it is never actually theirs, and stewards know they will one day turn in an account of their management of it. The sense of being a steward is an individual response to the insight that our life, our talents, our relationships, and all that we have are gifts entrusted to our care.

No matter what our level of material resources, if we truly have the sense that what we have is a gift, we will feel a responsibility, even a sense of urgency, to share with others some of what we have been given. (A sense of responsibility is not the same as a sense of obligation. See below for a fuller discussion of the importance of avoiding the language of obligation.) So stewards' gifts are motivated by gratitude and by a desire to fulfill their responsibility to share.

Stewardship formation and good fund-raising go together. Those who don't have the mentality of the steward need to be motivated to give. Those who understand themselves as stewards will often tithe or give some other percentage off the top, but they'll still want to direct their gifts where they think they'll do the most good. Stewards generally give because they feel a need to share, but no particular recipient church or organization is entitled to receive their gifts, and you can't take your donors for granted. My perception is that proportional givers will be slower to reduce or redirect their giving as a result of the normal frictions and conflicts of parish life, but careless leadership can alienate even tithers.

If you have it, you must give up the lazy attitude that assumes that your members are simply obliged to support your parish at the level that would solve your budget problems regardless of how well you're leading it. They aren't under that kind of obligation, whether they see themselves as owners or stewards. If they are owners, then you must do the kind of fund-raising that has thought carefully about what might motivate the membership to give. Stewards give because they feel an inner desire, or even a need, to give, but they don't necessarily need to give it to you. There are plenty of churches and charities out there: the money will tend to go to those who do a good job of articulating a vision for the institution and of taking nothing and no one for granted.

For a long time most church people have had the idea that "fund-raising" is bad, and "stewardship" is good. I want to rehabilitate the idea of fund-raising. Both fund-raising and stewardship formation are good and necessary in churches. I think it's necessary to distinguish the two, not because one is better than the other, but so that you can be clear about which one you're doing in a particular situation. Many churches use the word "stewardship" when they are really doing some rather crude fund-raising toward the needs of the budget. As you will see, there are several ways to do fund-raising; some are more effective than others. Most churches would do a much better job of raising the funds they need if they understood that fund-raising is perfectly all right and that it works best if it's done with careful preparation that provides people with a motivation to give.

Developing in people the sense that they are stewards, not owners, is another story.

The Catalyst for Transformation

When so much of our culture and society seems constructed on the sense of the individual's ownership of property and resources, how does one ever come to the insight that everything is a gift, and that one is a steward, not an owner? We don't get there simply by people telling us that we *should* feel that way. It comes, I think, not by growth, but from a kind of transformation. The transformation is something that happens within the individual, but almost always the transformation occurs through an individual's intense experiences as part of an institution. Because I believe that the reality is that life is a gift and we are stewards of it, it doesn't surprise me that the transformation can occur in secular as well as religious institutions.

The transformation can happen anywhere, but I think it usually happens in institutions that are aimed at transformation, and that give their participants a framework of meaning that can give them a way to interpret their experiences within the institution. Different kinds of institutions provide somewhat different structures of meaning, but I think the dynamic of the experience is the same across institutions.

Many people, including many active Christians, are more generous to the college or university they attended for four years than to any other charitable institution, including the parish they may have been part of for decades. This may be because they found their experience at college a transformative gift. The friendships, the intense discussions, the social networks, the exploration of oneself and the world — all these often occur at college during the years we pass from being adolescents to being adults. Despite the work and the money it takes to go to college, some come away feeling that all that they experienced was a tremendous, life-changing gift, beyond anything that they did to earn it. During those years people can discover who they are, what they're good at, and what their vocation is. Alumni may feel as though they were given their life and their future while at college, and they remain forever grateful to the institution through which those gifts were given.

Others experience a similar kind of transformation through military service. The armed services understand that people are frequently transformed by the intense relationships and the even more intense situations that soldiers can experience. The possibility of such a transformation is part of the military's advertising. When everything is at risk, you can come away from the chaos of violence realizing that every minute of life, regardless of the circumstances under which it is lived, is a precious gift.

And, of course, the transformation can occur within our congregations in all kinds of ways. When real forgiveness and reconciliation occur after strife, it's possible to understand in our bones that we don't earn God's favor: it's a gift. When intense experiences, such as births, bereavements, or personal or financial crises, occur in Christian communities, they are moments of vulnerability within a structure of meaning that can transform us, causing us first to know and feel that all that we have is a free gift from a loving God, and then to want to share what we've been given with the Giver and with others.

There doesn't have to be a crisis. In some people the transformation is gradual and quiet. The church has always provided the elements of transformation: the Scriptures, the Sacraments, and the life of the community. The life of the community includes the rhythm of corporate worship, opportunities to learn, chances to serve others outside the community, support for a personal devotional life, and lots of occasions to learn the difficulties and delights of maintaining relationships in the Body. These things change us over time if we give them even half a chance.

No set of circumstances or experiences necessarily results in converting us from owners to stewards. Many, many people never feel the change despite a lifetime of Christian practice. However, if we've felt the transformation, we will almost certainly feel a tenacious loyalty and generous gratitude to the institution that was the catalyst for it.

Priming the Pump

We can't force the conversion I've been talking about; it too is a gift. And yet there are ways to "seek the Lord while he wills to be found" (Isa. 55:6a). We cannot conjure or manipulate God — that's what religious magicians think they can do. We cannot earn God's favor by our works or buy it by our "generosity" — that was clarified by the Reformation, though the tendency continually reappears in all strains of Christianity, especially the ones that seem dominant at any moment. We can, however, prepare the ground. If we don't sow and water, it makes it more difficult for God to give the growth.

As I said in chapter 1, it's likely that you received the gift of faith in part because you were already acting *as if* you believed. You were coming to church and taking part in the life of the community while you were still longing to know God. In the same way, if you want to be a steward, begin the practice of proportional giving off the top. I think it's possible to act *as if* we were stewards even before we realize that we have received the gift of knowing that all that we have is a gift.

Let's start with desire. What do you want? What do you want from your life and from your participation in your parish?

Do you want to love God? Do you want God to fill you so there's no room for anxiety and suspicion? Do you long for an experience of God that changes your life? Do you want to get to the point where doing what you really want to do means doing what God wants? Do you want your heart to be with God? I think you do want these things. Why else would you be in church? Of course we want a life-transforming experience of God. Of course we want our hearts to be with God, and it's possible to act on that desire.

Put Your Money Where You Want Your Heart to Be

If you want your heart to be with God, here's a suggestion I've found very powerful in my own life. Put your money where you want your heart to be. Jesus said, "Where your treasure is, there will your heart be also." In other words, your heart follows your money, not the other way around. We think it's the other way around. We think we spend our money on the things that are important to us. Jesus is trying to tell us that those things have become important to us because they're what we spend our money on. Put your money where you want your heart to rest, and your heart will move there.

If you really want your heart to be with God — and I believe you do — then you might want to change how you give to your parish and to God's work accomplished by other charities. Don't treat your charitable giving as just another bill that has to be paid — or as one that doesn't get paid if there's not enough left over. Don't think of your gift as a tax or as club dues, and for heaven's sake, don't let it be just a tip that's less than you spend on lunches or commuting.

Make your gift a first-fruits offering. Fix a percentage in your heart and in your head, and give that percentage off the top to God every time money goes into your bank or into your hand. If you get money once a month, then give your percentage off the top once a month, and don't give the other weeks. If you get paid twice a month or every other week, then give at those times. Give weekly only if you receive money weekly. This is the first radical thing I'm suggesting. Stop giving by the week. Give to God at those times when God has given you something. And the second radical thing I'm suggesting is that you give back to God a percentage of what God has given you.

What percentage? We tithe. That's 10 percent of everything we receive, the first checks I write after receiving any money. If you want to try putting your money where you want your heart to rest, I strongly suggest you try giving at least 5 percent off the top back to God whenever God gives you anything. Giving God off the top a percentage of what God has given you is good, strong medicine for the heart. Ten percent is the recommended dose. Five percent is a therapeutic dose, but giving back to God any percentage off the top — 2.5 percent or 3 percent or 4 percent — is better for your heart than giving any set amount that is not off the top and that has no relationship to your income.

It's easy to figure what percentage you're already giving. Divide what you give by your income. If what you're giving works out to be less than 3 percent of your income — and some find it works out to less than 1 percent — then please just try giving God off the top three or five cents of every dollar God gives you. You *can* give God a nickel off the top of every dollar you get. You'll do just fine with all your other obligations. In fact, the more anxious you are now about money, the more important it is to change how you give. Put your money where you want your heart to rest. Your heart will move there, and you'll be much less anxious about money because you'll be trusting God's promises, and that's the essence of faith.

What do you put on a pledge card? I put an estimate of what I think my percentage will result in, turn in the pledge card, and forget the estimate. I concentrate on the percentage. It's always turned out all right.

This will change your life. You may think that paying your bills is the least religious thing you do. Percentage giving off the top begins to change all of that, because each time you sit down to deal with your money, the first thing you do is to make a thank offering to God that is in proportion to what God has just given you. It changes how you think about your life and what you have. It turns dealing with your money into an act of faith, part of our worship in spirit and in truth. It makes it far more likely that you will come to understand yourself as a steward of God's free gifts, rather than the owner of what you have.

Here's one way things change. If we think we are owners and that it's all up to us, it's easy for money to become the end. Getting enough money can become our life's goal. Well, if money is the end, then it's also easy for people and relationships to become means to that end. Proportional giving off the top, at least in my experience, changes that almost immediately. Especially if the percentage you've set is more than you really think you can possibly afford, almost with the very first check, things change. You realize that money is a tool: it's a means; it's not the end. Relationships and people, particularly our relationship with God, can become the end. And almost immediately you realize that it's not just up to you. God is in it with you. You've decided to rely on God's promises, and that is the essence of Christian faith. You come to experience what St. Paul is talking about: "work out your own salvation with fear and trembling; for God is at work in you, both to will and to work his own good pleasure" (Phil. 2:12b–13).

Whether we think of money as an end or a means, in fact our money is always a tool, and it's a tool that is always working on us. Most of the time, especially when we think getting money is the end, money works on us by making us feel more anxious and more driven. However, giving a percentage back to God of whatever God has given us turns our money into a tool that is in service to our relationship with God and to our spiritual transformation. Giving back to God a percentage of what God has given us helps us really trust God with our whole life. It helps us come to *want* to live the way God wants us to live. I'm quite serious. When I began to tithe as an adult, it changed my life. I believe I can predict that this can change your life as well.

Here's some of the evidence on which I base that prediction. Recently in a small but dynamic parish in our diocese, twenty-one of the forty-plus pledgers decided to switch from a weekly dollar pledge to proportional giving off the top. Some calculated their current level of giving as a percentage and didn't increase the amount given; some went to 3 percent or 5 percent. The priest invited those who had adopted this practice to come to occasional group meetings to discuss the experience. She invited me to the first meeting in late winter. Sixteen of the twenty-one came, a diverse group of professionals, freelancers, and artists ranging in age from early twenties on up. After only a few months of practicing proportional giving off the top, all present had something to say about how the experience had already begun to change them. Some were less anxious about money. Some freelancers related the commonly heard experience of not only feeling less anxious, but actually having received more offers of work. Others had experienced a change in priorities: things they had been spending money on had now become less important. Many spoke of a deepened faith and a greater trust in God's love and care.

I think if you try giving this way for a period of time, you'll wonder why no one ever suggested this to you before. And I doubt you'll ever go back.

From Obligation to Opportunity

You'll have noticed that I haven't presented only the tithe as acceptable. I think it is vital to encourage people to give a percentage — any percentage — off the top. I'm convinced that if someone changes from giving $25 a week to even 2 percent off the top, the crucial change will have been made. I concede that the power of the experience is in proportion to the, well, proportion of income given. It is thrilling to leap into water whose depth and temperature are unknown, only to discover that, not only is everything fine, but that it's exactly where you've always wanted to be. You might not experience the full thrill if you wade in from the shallow end, yet I'd rather coax people into the shallows than for them never to try the water.

I know tithing is not even considered a desirable goal in some quarters. It seems unfair to the poor. We're accustomed to a progressive tax system. We're more than accustomed to it; many of us feel, as our Lord said, that much is required from those to whom much has been given. Tithing is regressive in that sense.

I think the objection misses the point. Tithing is precisely *not* a tax, though our teaching of tithing as an institutional norm or requirement feeds the view that it is a tax, and that's the reason I do not use that kind of language in speaking of proportional giving. Proportional giving off the top is both an expression of our longing for faith and a response of faith and thanksgiving for God's good gifts.

Those of us who lead the institution — the ligaments, as it were, in the Body of Christ — are sometimes subject to a kind of "institutional fallacy." In speaking with clergy about proportional giving, I've sometimes heard, "We do that — 10 percent of our budget goes to outreach," as if individuals don't need to think about proportional giving because the institution's budget is doing it for them. The institution is the setting, the context in which the transformation of the lives of the members of the Body can take place. However, the life of the institution can't be a substitute for transformation in the lives of the members.

Then there's the objection I hear in every meeting with parish leaders, "You can't ask people in this parish to give more; most of our members are on fixed incomes." My experience of fixed incomes leads me even more strongly to invite people in all economic circumstances to move to proportional giving and tithing. It fell to my mother to bring us up because my father died, leaving four children under the age of ten. She raised us, tithed, and taught us to tithe on the very fixed income my father had left. No matter the level at which your income is fixed, you can tithe or give another percentage off the top if only your heart is moved to do so.

Don't patronize those with less by telling them they're excused from the life-changing blessings of proportional giving. It is certainly significant that Jesus didn't tell the widow to keep her mite because she couldn't afford to give it away. And if he had said that, how would it have made her feel?

From Stewardship to Fund-Raising

Stewardship is the understanding that we are not owners; we hold God's gifts in trust. I believe that proportional giving off the top is inextricably linked with the sense of being a steward, not an owner. Being converted from a "self-made man who worships his creator" to a conscious steward is a transformation that occurs within the individual in lots of different and unpredictable ways through one's participation in the life of the institution. The transformation certainly involves more than money, but the transformation of our self-understanding will necessarily transform our relationship to our money.

Even when that transformation has occurred, even if your pews are full of stewards giving proportionally off the top, you still need to do a good job of fund-raising. Good fund-raising is not just saying, "We need more money." Good fund-raising is thinking carefully about why you want the money and why anyone, whether owner or steward, would be motivated to give it to you. So let's turn to the kinds of giving people do and the ways of asking for their support for your institution.

The Three Kinds of Giving

There are three ways people give to the support of their parish or any charitable institution. We'll mention them here and examine each in more detail in this chapter.

To begin with, there are gifts that come from the donors' current income. This is the kind of giving we're most familiar with; it's what most not-for-profits call *annual giving*. Most of us know it as "pledging," or "taking envelopes." It's our normal weekly or monthly giving. Annual giving is called that for several reasons. First, usually what we give to the church in this way comes from our current annual income. Second, annual giving is almost always directed in support of the annual operating budget. Normally the operating budget provides for the recurring — one might even say relentless — expenses of the basic program of the congregation, such as salaries, benefits, the amount due the judicatory and the national office, education, music, outreach, utilities, and insurance.

Finally, most not-for-profits call this kind of giving annual giving because gifts are solicited and made once a year. That pattern of giving is most certainly not what I'm talking about here. When I use the term "annual giving" with regard to churches, I mean those gifts that generally come from our current income and that generally are used for current operating expenses.

The second kind is *capital giving*. Parishes usually mount capital campaigns to build new buildings, to upgrade or restore existing buildings, or to create or add to an endowment. Capital giving is called that for two reasons. First, the purpose of a capital campaign is never to pay current bills, but to make some addition or improvement to the long-term assets, or "capital" of the parish — the buildings or the investments. Second, the major gifts on which the success of capital campaigns almost always depends usually come not from the donors' current income, but from the wealth, or capital, the donor has accumulated.

The final kind of gift — and it is often someone's final gift — comes from the donor's estate. These end-of-life gifts are what is usually meant by *planned giving* because the donor decides to make this kind of gift often years before actually making it. There are all kinds of ways of making planned gifts. You can bequeath an amount of money in your will, or you can leave real estate or a percentage of your residual estate to the church. You can make your parish the beneficiary or partial beneficiary of a life insurance policy. You can set up a gift annuity or a charitable remainder trust. In most cases, planned gifts have two characteristics. First, the donor has decided to make the gift in advance of making it. Second, the death of the donor typically triggers the actual making of the gift.

Asking for Money

In outlining the three kinds of giving, I have also called attention to the three sources of money — one's current income, one's accumulated assets, and one's estate. The motivations people have for giving from these three sources differ, and that's part of what we talk about here.

As I've said, your parish is not entitled to its members' money. You need to think clearly about what you're asking for, why you are asking for it, and what motivation the people you're asking have for responding. And most importantly, you can't take your donors for granted. That means asking instead of just assuming. It means saying thank you. And of course it means complete transparency and accountability in how you handle every penny that passes through the parish's books.

St. James could have been talking about congregational leaders' efforts to solicit donations from their membership when he wrote, "You do not have, because you do not ask. You ask and do not receive, because you ask wrongly . . . " (James 4:2b–3). If your annual pledge drive consists solely of a letter like the one you sent last year with a pledge card enclosed, don't be surprised if the results are lackluster. As we say in New York, if you don't ask, you don't get. And some ways of asking are more effective than others.

Watch Your Language, and Here's Why .

We're about to come to the different ways of asking for money, but first a word about the language I suggest you use. It is my deep conviction that people do what they want to do — or at least what they think they want to do. People will not do something they don't want to do for very long even when they're under surveillance. Those of us who "do our duty" can attest that we do it not primarily because we are *supposed* to do our duty, but because we have learned to *want* to do our duty. The point is that we are in the most fundamental sense motivated by desire, not by fear or by a sense of obligation. Our desires may not be consistent; our desires may not be in our best interests; indeed, the desires that motivate some of our actions may not even be what we really want. Nevertheless, it is always desire that drives us.

That ability to desire, to be able to will something, rather than act simply on instinct shaped by experience, is a gift from God. God made us, as St. Augustine said, so that "our hearts are restless until they rest in Thee." God is the satisfaction of our true desire. God wants us to aim the desires of our heart straight toward his heart of love. The Christian life is discovering whom we truly want, and discovering how to order our actions to keep our desires aimed at the target for which they were made.

We Christians are about conversion, not compliance. The law is about compliance with the rules, and the law provides rewards for obedience and punishments for misbehavior. The Christian life is not about forcing ourselves to obey the law; it's about discovering what Jews call "simchat Torah," the joy of the law, the delight that comes from *wanting* to do what God wants. The same thought is expressed in the Collect for Proper 25, " . . . and, that we may obtain what you promise, make us love what you command . . . " (BCP, p. 235). The real aim is not that we *do* what God commands, but that we *love* it, and so do it because we *want* to.

We are not capable on our own of healing our wills so that we really and truly want for ourselves what God wants for us. In this life salvation is about the healing of our wills, redirecting the trajectory of our desire so that all the desires of our hearts and minds center in what God would have us do.

The language of obligation is a kind of shorthand that is easy to use, but the sense of obligation is not the end we're aiming at. I've used the language of obligation plenty so far in this book. Again and again I've said that you need to, ought to, have to do certain things and that you must and should do other things. Maybe it hasn't always been clear that it is shorthand, but I hope to make it so now. I think you *want* the congregation entrusted to your charge to thrive. Everything I've said has been aimed at helping you achieve the goal I believe you want to achieve — a healthy congregation of Christians whose lives God in Christ is transforming through the work of the Holy Spirit in your community.

It's all right to use the shorthand of obligation as long as we never lose sight of the real goal — making it possible for people to do the right thing because they have come to want to. If we're not able to explain to people why they would ever *want* to do something, we won't make a great deal of progress in getting them to do it just because we say that the Bible and the church say they *should*.

I would counsel everyone in Christian leadership to avoid the language of obligation and concentrate instead on the language of desire — especially when talking of money. The point is not to convince people that they *should* be doing some good thing that they aren't doing; the point is surely to get people to realize that at a deep level they *want* to do that good thing. Try taking the shoulds and the oughts out of your discourse, and you'll see how much we use the language of obligation. It can be difficult at first to rephrase what you want to say into the language of desire, but I think you'll find that it's worth the effort.

The Five Institutional Pitches

Leaders of institutions usually speak of the institution when asking for money. That is completely appropriate when doing institutional fund-raising. I think that all the ways there are of asking people for money on behalf of the institution can be grouped in five broad categories. I'll outline what I call the five institutional pitches, starting with the least effective.

The sky is falling, the sky is falling

There are several reasons why *The sky is falling* is not an effective motivator, and they are fairly obvious. First, people can't stay on high alert for very long. If the sky is always falling, people will find a way to live normally while dodging the pieces that tumble down. Second, *The sky is falling* is an admission of defeat by the leadership. Unless it involves some truly unforeseeable disaster, the "emergency" is probably a failure to plan, and a lot of people will recognize that. Third, *The sky is falling* usually masks some other motivation, because it's generally not the case that the sky is really falling. Finally, *The sky is falling* is an approach a true leader will not use, because if the sky really is falling, then there's no future, and as we've seen, leadership is about the future. People don't give to organizations that run endless going-out-of-business sales, and people don't trust stores that run permanent close-out sales but never close.

Although this is the least effective way of asking for money, a fair number of people rely on this approach, and at least in some cases I think I may know why. In one parish the wealthiest member was also for years in charge of drafting the budget. He always made sure there was a deficit of some size, possibly by regulating the size of his pledge. This allowed him to keep people's anxiety fairly high, and it gave him a great deal of control over a parish that he also loved a great deal. That may have been the point.

If someone in your congregation is using *The sky is falling* to exercise control over other people or for some other less than praiseworthy motive, try to figure out a way to get that to stop. Stay away from this approach unless it's really true. And even if it's really true, use it very sparingly. Find something that will motivate people to want to give.

Come help us pay our bills

This is perhaps the most frequently used appeal by leaders who are anxious about money. Despite the spectacular ineffectiveness of this approach's evangelistic appeal, it is behind lots of discussions of "church growth," as in, "We need more people in this parish so we can make the budget." Although it is a commonplace to say that people don't give to budgets, the budget need is what most people talk the most about at pledge season. *Come help us pay our bills* is just a needs-based appeal that doesn't provide people much of any motivation to give.

Come help us pay our bills is the approach that is behind any pitch that simply asks people to raise their pledge by so much a week, or that spells out a "fair share" pledge. Anything that turns giving into dues or taxes is based on this approach. It's an approach everyone can understand, but that doesn't make it effective. As I've said, many churches rely on *Come help us pay our bills* every year as the main pitch in what they call their stewardship campaign. Because many people think that stewardship formation is really a mask for raising funds for the budget, the more you do bad fund-raising instead of stewardship, the more you will convince your people that there is no such thing as stewardship; there's only bad fund-raising. You will give them some pretty compelling reasons for thinking that "all the church cares about is my money." In the end you will be doing them a great disservice, and their spiritual growth can't help but be stunted.

Come help us pay our bills is not effective fund-raising; it certainly isn't stewardship formation.

However, there is certainly a need to talk about the budget in certain contexts and to give people the right amount of information at the appropriate times about the congregation's finances. It is appropriate that there be full disclosure of all parish finances at the annual meeting. (I wish it weren't necessary to add that I hope you will make sure this information is presented in such a way that people can easily understand it.) The monthly financial reports given to the governing board can be posted. However, that is more information than most of your members probably want — and given some of the financial reports I've seen, those reports may not be presented in the most user-friendly format. The kind of information that is appropriate might be something like the following in the monthly newsletter:

Last month	
Offerings	$11,587
Other operating income	2,850
Total operating income	$14,437
(Operating expenses)	(15,742)
Surplus/(deficit)	($1,305)

Or this in the weekly bulletin:

Offering last week	$2,857
One week's budgeted expenses	$3,400

Many congregations have, or used to have, a board in the nave with information like this:

Attendance last week	109
Attendance a year ago	117
Offering last week	$2,539
Offering a year ago	$2,248

Manageable amounts of pertinent information disseminated regularly give the people the sense that their leaders are accountable and that they are faithfully discharging their responsibilities. Although *Come help us pay our bills* is not a great motivator for people to give, the appropriate amount of financial information in the appropriate form (and only you can define what is appropriate in your own context) is a crucial part of the openness about financial matters that allows members to trust their leadership. And that trust is essential if the leaders want to motivate giving.

Team spirit

This approach includes all appeals that are based on the life of the community or the congregational family. The presence of a thermometer with a goal is always a sign of the team spirit approach. *Team spirit* is often blended with *Come help us pay our bills* as a way of softening the latter's bluntness, as in, "We need all of us to increase our pledges by $10 a week, and this is such a warm, committed group that I know we can do this." *Team spirit* is all about "We can do this, guys. We're all in this together. We've got a great place here. It takes all of us to keep it." All of these sentiments have a useful and appropriate, though limited, place in any appeal for funds. *Team spirit* is a strong motivator in planned giving, as in "You can ensure that this community that has been so important to you will be here for future generations." That same appeal also plays an effective role in many capital campaigns.

A particularly effective way of incorporating *Team spirit* into your annual pledge drive is for all the members of the governing board to make their pledges before any pledges are solicited from the congregation. The leadership then introduces the pledge drive to the congregation by including an announcement like this: "The clergy staff and every member of the vestry and the treasurer have already made their pledges for the coming year. The total pledged by these seventeen people for next year is $62,000."

Team spirit adds to our fund-raising efforts an appeal to our esprit de corps and to our gung-ho commitment. It has a great deal of effectiveness and this limitation: as we remember from high-school pep rallies, *Team spirit* simply assumes that we all agree that the game is important and that it's important for our team to do well. In order to inspire people at a deep level, church leaders can't simply assume all that. People will want their leaders to be able to explain the point of the "game" and of the congregation's role in it. That ability is part of being prepared to give "an accounting for the hope that is in you" (1 Pet. 3:15).

NPR/PBS

This pitch comes in two parts, just as it does on public broadcasting. During the appeal for pledges the pitch is, "We believe you like the programming we offer. We believe you like it because we know you watch or listen to it. If you want us to be able to continue to offer it, please support us." During the rest of the year the pitch is repeated in the context of gratitude: "This show and shows like this are what your gifts make possible. Thank you, members."

This is an effective appeal. It works; that's why it is the basis of all those pledge drives on radio and TV. It is certainly a consumerist appeal, and that is one of its limitations. But before we disparage it on those grounds, let's acknowledge that those who market to the consumer are at least thinking about the needs, preferences, and desires of the consumer. Public broadcasting does not take its audience for granted. It thinks about what its audience would like without pandering (usually), and it constantly makes the connection between the institution's ability to provide what its membership base wants and the membership support that makes it possible.

If I have not yet convinced you of the need to eschew the language of obligation, take a lesson from public broadcasting. Public radio and TV stations tried guilt and found it didn't work. In the early pledge drives, I recall, there was incomprehension, frustration, and even resentment at the stations when the public didn't respond adequately. "You *should* give," the hosts would say. "You watch or listen to our programming, so you *ought to* support it." If you listen to or watch the appeals now, you will hear very little, if any, of that. The appeal is to the potential member's desire to keep the programs on the air, and they say "thank you" over and over again. Lots of churches could learn a great deal from this.

A common pledge program in congregations solicits the congregation's ideas and priorities through a planning conference, puts a price tag to the things the congregation would like to do, and calculates the percentage of self-reported average or median household income that would be necessary for members to give to make those ideas a reality. That's a form of the *NPR/PBS* approach, and it works pretty well. In his book *One-Minute Stewardship Sermons* (Morehouse Publishing, 1997), the Reverend Charles Cloughen Jr. recommends every week during the announcements briefly connecting the congregation's ability to fulfill its mission with the congregants' gifts of time, abilities, and money. And in making that connection the pastor thanks the members for their generosity. This is *NPR/PBS* at its very best; by all means I recommend adopting a similar practice.

NPR/PBS is a very common part of most capital campaign pitches as well. When you get the congregation to buy in on the campaign's goals, *NPR/PBS* is the backbone of the pitch fleshed out by *Team spirit:* "You've told us you'd like the congregation to be able to do these things. For St. Swithin's to be able to get there, we ask for everyone's support."

Even as I write about it, though, the consumerism inherent in the appeal starts to grate a bit. I don't think there's a way to use *NPR/PBS* without saying things like, "If *you* want *us* to be able...," and "*We* can to this because of *your* support." That's fine for public broadcasting: *we* are indeed consumers of what *they* broadcast. It's pernicious in parish life to set up any kind of "we the provider/you the consumer" mentality. On the other hand, it is very useful to be able to talk about all that the congregation is able to do because of its members' support. It is very important for the members to know what their gifts make possible. And it's most important for the leadership to say "thank you."

Catch the vision

There is no doubt that leaders with a compelling vision of both what the institution can be and what individuals can become through their participation in the institution make the most effective appeal for support of the institution. Leaders with that kind of vision can build new congregations from scratch and turn parishes on the brink of disaster into thriving centers of worship, formation, and outreach.

The principal drawback is that it isn't possible to pretend that there is such a vision where it doesn't exist. Thinking or saying you have a vision doesn't make it so. Getting through the year or meeting an unexpected crisis is not a vision. Keeping the ship from sinking is not a vision. Managing decline or holding the fort is not a vision. Trying implicitly or explicitly to re-create a past golden age is not a vision. Denying current trends is not a vision.

If you realize that your leadership doesn't have a vision right now, you certainly don't need to despair. The realization that you don't have a vision for the future is an important place to begin. The first move toward developing a vision is to catch a sense of the future. What could that future look like in our circumstances? What goals could we set? What steps could we take? How could we redirect our efforts and our resources in order to move toward that future?

The Scripture, the liturgy, and the Sacraments have always been the foundation for a compelling vision. The leadership can do an effective job of revitalizing congregational life in the way many congregations have known for centuries — through a presentation of the gospel that speaks to people's lives. I can virtually guarantee that you can improve annual giving by dropping all language of guilt and obligation. Offer instead some concrete initiatives, however modest, that can move the congregation into the future. Talk incessantly about that future; point out over and over any signs there may be that any part of that future is coming about; and concentrate on a combination of *NPR/PBS* and *Team spirit* with the appropriate amounts and kinds of financial information discussed in *Come help us pay our bills.*

The faithful perseverance of committed leaders who consider the aspirations of the congregation, who love their members and hold themselves accountable to them, and who present prudent and thoughtful next steps for the congregation to take into the future God is preparing for them — all this is the kind of leadership on which Christ has built the church. You *can* articulate a vision for your congregation. If you realize that the day-to-day-ness of congregational life and its inevitable frictions have dimmed your eyes, that realization is itself important. Call on the assistance of someone at your judicatory or national office. Find a sympathetic outsider who can help you evaluate your situation. Consult with that person about ways to rekindle your desire to be transformed by Christ's love and to offer your congregation as a place where that transformation can occur again and again in the lives of its members.

Building on the Foundation

The foundation for all giving by your members is the stewardship formation you do all the time and the way you approach your congregation's annual giving. If you never speak of money, and your pledge drive consists solely of one standard letter that urges people to give because the sky is falling, it will be difficult for you to mount a successful capital campaign, and you will likely receive few planned gifts.

On the other hand, leaders with a compelling vision will speak of giving money frequently, not as an obligation that must be met, but as a series of life-transforming opportunities to be generous stewards. They will give the members both institutional and personal motivations to give. Such leaders will almost certainly have a dream for the facilities, and it will ignite energy for capital campaigns to raise endowments and to enable the buildings to house and support the mission. They'll inspire the membership to want to see the blessings of the congregation preserved for future generations, and planned gifts will start to come.

Capital and planned gift campaigns are built on the foundation that the leadership has laid for good personal and institutional stewardship. The foundation for good personal stewardship means commending — and modeling — proportional giving and emphasizing the effective ways of appealing for funds on behalf of the institution. The institutional foundation involves matters we've touched on previously, including accountability in handling money, prudence in managing the long-term investments, foresight in funding the capital reserve, and restraint in relying on other people's money. Only when these matters are being tended to can leaders hope for good results from a capital or planned giving effort.

Capital Campaigns

A capital campaign is not a brief fund-raising drive to take care of some relatively minor need. A capital campaign typically involves a major effort to raise an amount that is some multiple of your annual pledges. You'll be asking people to make a significant commitment to the capital campaign and very likely to pay that commitment over three to five years. The capital campaigns and planned giving efforts that you will build on the foundation of good personal stewardship are almost prefabricated structures. Especially with regard to capital campaigns there is a protocol, a set pattern to how they work. If you follow the pattern, you are very likely to have a successful capital campaign. If you try to invent your own model, or if you try to cut parts out of the pattern, you are very likely to be disappointed.

One priest expressed reservations about a cookie-cutter approach to a capital drive he was contemplating. I observed, I hope helpfully, that if your goal is to make cookies, it's more useful to use a cookie-cutter than to try to cut each one out with a knife.

My observations here are not intended to be a manual for how to do a capital campaign on your own. *Do not try to do a capital campaign on your own.* What follows is aimed mostly at trying to explain why it is a good idea to follow the path that thousands of churches and other not-for-profits have trod before you. I encourage you not to deviate from that path to the right or to the left.

Campaigns look backward or forward

Institutions generally undertake capital campaigns to deal with the buildings. Sometimes the goal of the campaign has to do with establishing or adding to the endowment, but most capital campaigns are for the buildings, and the campaign either looks backward or looks forward.

What I call backward-looking campaigns are those that deal with deferred maintenance or with the replacement of elements that have reached the end of their useful lives. The roof needs to be replaced; the siding needs to be painted or replaced; the stone has to be repointed because water is getting in through the walls. I call these backward-looking campaigns because they are aimed at catching up. If things had been going better, or if the leadership had been planning better, there would be capital reserve funds that would have been able to take care of these things along the way. For whatever reason, you didn't or couldn't accumulate the necessary reserves, so it is necessary to have a capital campaign.

A forward-looking capital campaign has to do with building something new, or renovating an existing building to adapt it to current needs, or upgrading your plant to bring it up to present-day codes and standards. Ramps, lifts, and elevators that make your buildings fully accessible, air conditioning the plant, installing a professionally designed sound or lighting system, adding a wing, historically appropriate restorations — all these are examples of what I would call a forward-looking campaign.

A capital campaign is often a combination of elements that look forward and others that deal with deferred maintenance. I probably don't need to say that in general people feel better about forward-looking campaigns. In such campaigns the basis of the appeal can be the congregation's vision for the future, and, if the leaders handle it right, they can generate a great deal of excitement about what the new or renovated spaces can do. In other words, the appeal can use the more effective of the institutional pitches — *Catch the vision* and *NPR/PBS* with the right amount of *Team Spirit*. A campaign that must deal primarily with catch-up work will necessarily be based more on the less effective end of the spectrum — *Come help us pay our bills* and even *The sky is falling* with as much *Team spirit* as you can muster.

I think it's a good idea to have some forward-looking elements in the campaign even if the bulk of it is catch-up work.

Raising endowment funds is generally a forward-looking element. Usually there's a vision of how the endowment will propel the congregation's mission in the future. However, if you're trying to replace an endowment that has been depleted through overspending or the ravages of inflation, you need to make sure that you have mended your ways and rebuilt the trust of the membership. They're not likely to give you more money if they think you'll repeat an unfortunate pattern.

The need for professional counsel

A capital campaign has to bring together two amounts of money that aren't necessarily related — (1) the amount you need to accomplish the work you envision, and (2) the amount it's possible for you to raise. Many campaigns have been disappointments because the two haven't been brought together well.

The seed of a capital campaign is almost invariably the need. There are things that have to be done, or there are things people would like to see done, or a combination of the two. You get an idea from engineers or architects of what the projects would cost. You get a sense of whether a campaign is possible. Are you in shape to do a campaign? Do you have the trust of your members? Do they think you're doing a good job with your stewardship of the resources? Do they share your vision?

As soon as you have an informal sense that it's time for a capital campaign, and as soon as you have an idea of what you'd like to do and some sense of what it would cost, *you hire professional counsel.*

Let me say that again in case you missed it. *You hire professional counsel.*

From here on I want only to describe what the professional counsel is likely to do. If anything here differs from the advice the counsel gives you, ignore my words, and listen to the expert you have retained. There are several firms out there, and they aren't hard to find. Take the recommendations of the staff of your judicatory or denomination about whom to contact. Check the references of the prospective fund-raising counsel. You want to interview more than one firm. Don't look only at which one might charge the least. Go with the one you trust and with whom you think you can work the best. Don't go with anybody who wants a percentage of what you raise. Reputable fund-raising counsel will charge you a fee based on the amount of work involved. Pay the fee without grumbling. I assure you that the total you will raise with professional counsel less the fee will far exceed what you would raise without the assistance of the counsel. And because you're paying the counsel, you'll be more likely to do what the counsel directs.

Talk to the counsel about your wish list of projects. Allow the counsel to guide you about how to solicit the congregation's involvement in coming up with the final list of projects.

Don't cut corners. The fund-raising counsel will probably want to do a feasibility study before recommending a dollar goal for the campaign. Do the feasibility study. During the feasibility study, the counsel will talk to a sampling of your donor base. The counsel will be testing both how much potential donors are *able* to give and how much they'll be *willing* to give toward the projects that are contemplated. When the counsel suggests a goal, don't imagine that you can increase it just because what you need to do costs more. Trust me, and trust the counsel. What you can raise from the campaign will almost certainly be the amount the counsel tells you is feasible. The counsel has experience here, and you'll do well to be guided by it.

The counsel also has an incentive to discern the largest goal that can successfully be met. The goal and the results of your campaign will be on the firm's resume. The counsel's incentive is to set as the goal the biggest number that can be met or oversubscribed. You also have an incentive to make sure the campaign successfully meets the dollar goal set, even if it's not all the money you need. An unsuccessful capital campaign sets the community back. Generally, it will be quite a while before you can mount another campaign after one that has failed.

A capital campaign is almost always based on a pyramid of gifts. The 80/20 rule applies as much here as anywhere else: the bulk of the money will typically come from a small group of donors. However, everyone's gift and everyone's participation is important. And don't worry about the effect of a capital campaign on your annual giving efforts. A well-run campaign in a healthy congregation to fund goals that the members are excited about will almost always have a positive effect on annual giving. People find they can give more; what's more, they find that giving money away to projects they're committed to is one of life's most pleasurable experiences. Your annual pledge campaigns in the years following a successful capital campaign are likely to make everyone feel even better.

Once you know what you can raise, work with the counsel to define exactly what work the campaign will be aimed at funding. Bring the amount you need into harmony with the amount you will be able to raise. Those projects will probably be a combination of things that need to be done and things the members would like to have done. The counsel will help you prepare the material you need to "make the case" to your potential donors.

The rest is doing what needs to be done in the way it needs to be done. I don't mean it isn't a lot of work, but there's a set form to what the work is, and the professional counsel you have retained knows what to do, when to do it, and how to do it. An unsuccessful capital campaign can shake a congregation's confidence for years. A successful campaign can be the springboard for some amazing ministry in the years after the campaign. You can do it. And you might be amazed.

Planned Giving

The Minister of the Congregation is directed to instruct the people, from time to time, about the duty of Christian parents to make prudent provision for the well-being of their families, and of all persons to make wills, while they are in health, arranging for the disposal of their temporal goods, not neglecting, if they are able, to leave bequests for religious and charitable uses.

—Book of Common Prayer, page 445

There it is in black and white, for Episcopalians anyway. The Book of Common Prayer is considered part of the Constitution of the Episcopal Church, and the rubrics of the Prayer Book have the force of canon law. If the rectors, vicars, and priests-in-charge of Episcopal congregations are not conducting some kind of planned giving effort, they're neglecting part of their jobs. It's as if they were failing to conduct services on the Lord's Day.

Many have observed that we are experiencing an enormous transfer of wealth in this country. The Episcopal Church Foundation estimates that in the next twenty years about $50 *trillion* in assets will pass from one generation to the next. From the mail I receive and the ads I encounter on radio and TV, institutions of higher learning, private schools, hospitals, libraries, community service agencies, and public broadcasting stations all seem well aware of this fact. Yet the churches where many of these people worship every week and in which the funerals of these people will be held seem oblivious to it.

Here is at least one place where the graying of the mainline churches should be a boon. I do not mean to be flippant. Of all people, we Christians should not feel self-conscious about addressing the fact that we all will die. For us death is not the last word, so talk of death doesn't need to be avoided. Death can be part of the conversation we have with one another precisely because the bond God has established with us in baptism is indissoluble. We can speak of these things because we know that "to your faithful people, O Lord, life is changed, not ended; and, when our mortal body lies in death, there is prepared for us a dwelling place eternal in the heavens" (BCP, p. 382).

And yet we fail to give our members the opportunity to help ensure that the church that has meant so much to them can thrive so that it can mean as much to future generations. We don't talk to them about how their bequest or other planned gift could strengthen the witness and the presence of the parish where so many of the milestone events of their lives have been celebrated.

Here we see the largest failure of vision of the leadership of our churches. Why would the university where we spent four years of our lives — formative though those years were — have a larger claim on us than the parish where we worshiped for forty years and where our children were baptized and married? The university doesn't have a greater claim, but the university's Planned Giving Office knows how important it is (1) to do some preparation before they ask, (2) to ask in a focused way that tells the donors that their gifts are important, and (3) to treat the gifts with respect.

Our members deserve no less from us. We are missing a great opportunity to minister to our members by not asking them to make planned gifts that will benefit the church. By not asking when others are asking, we communicate to them that their gifts are less important to us than they are to other organizations. By asking haphazardly and without any preparation, we show our members a level of disrespect. By spending the bequests we might receive to plug a budget deficit we show a level of carelessness, if not contempt, for that final act of devotion. By that cavalier treatment, we certainly communicate to the rest of our members that we probably won't show any greater care for their final gift. How surprising is it that our members make gifts to those who will appreciate them more?

It is fitting that the final discussion in this book should be about planned gifts. The solicitation of planned gifts and the care we take of them when our members make them are an expression of our vision of the future. Carelessness in this matter is almost certainly either self-centeredness (what I'm doing now matters more than preparing for my successors) or a lack of faith that there will be a future. We owe it to ourselves, our members, and our successors to do better.

Your judicatory or denomination has planned giving resources. Get them, review them, and lay the necessary groundwork to make yourself a worthy recipient of someone's last gift. No matter how informal or elaborate your planned giving effort is, here are some things to consider. The discussion of capital campaigns assumed that you would engage professional counsel. My discussion of planned giving assumes you are going to make full use of the resources available to you from your judicatory or denominational headquarters, and that you will hire *and pay for* the professional counsel you need to do it right. These are just some basics to help get you pointed in the right direction.

1. Make a policy about what you'll do with planned gifts, and let people know about it.

If you begin to think through a policy about what to do with bequests and planned gifts, you'll probably realize that it needs to be something other than "plug the budget deficit," or "spend it on whatever we feel like at the time." As I've indicated, I strongly suggest that you treat all bequests as permanent additions to your endowment. And I suggest that the bulk of the funds you use from the endowment go to the capital maintenance of the buildings and to outreach. Do not rely on dead people's money to pay the oil bill, the insurance premium, or the salaries of the clergy. Let the people who are benefiting from those things pay for them from their proportional gifts to the annual budget. Let the financial legacies of past generations keep sound the buildings left to you by past generations. Whether or not you take my recommendation, agree on some policy for the use of planned gifts, and then let your members know of that policy.

2. Adopt investment guidelines and a disciplined structure.

If, as I hope, you decide that all planned gifts will be treated as principal contributions to a perpetual endowment, be sure you have in place how you will treat the funds you invest. All funds remain under the control of the vestry or governing board, but you want to set up a bit of a buffer so that the board won't be able easily to dip into principal to plug a future budget deficit. Setting up that buffer and explaining to the members how that buffer will protect the funds is a crucial part of building the congregation's confidence that you will indeed treat their final gift with the respect it deserves. If your judicatory or denomination has a managed investment vehicle that sets and monitors the allocation of assets, calculates the drawdown, and sends it to you, your guidelines can be quite simple. Buy into that managed investment vehicle. If a solution like that isn't available to you, you can set up the buffer you need internally. Appoint an investment committee or an endowment committee, adopt the guidelines described in chapter 3, and be sure you abide by them.

The idea is not to create a separate organization that controls the funds apart from the legal fiduciaries of your congregation. The point, rather, is to create a structure that helps everyone maintain some discipline around the endowment. The governing board would adopt the investment guidelines and the spending rate. The investment committee would implement those decisions by overseeing the asset allocation within the parameters of the guidelines. The investment committee would calculate the amount available each year according to the adopted guidelines and tell the budget committee or the governing board what that amount is.

Congregations are usually very good at observing their customs. You want to create a simple custom of restraint around the investments, as in, "The way we do it here is to maintain an asset allocation and take out a percentage that goes into our capital reserve fund." That will go a long way to prevent people from coming to rely in unhealthy ways on other people's money.

3. Ask.

Talk about it. Put items in the newsletter and the weekly bulletin. Speak of it. You've let people know how you'll use the money; let people know what the possible gifts are. It's more than bequests. People can make gifts of stock; they'll get an acknowledgment of the market value on the day of the gift and avoid capital gains tax.

People can give gifts of real estate. The donor should be prepared for the church to sell the property unless it makes compelling sense to hold it. The tax deduction is usually based on the appraisal commissioned by the donor on a date near the day of the closing. People can make the church the beneficiary of any assets left in a retirement account like an IRA, a 403(b), or a 401(k) plan. The church can be a full or partial beneficiary of a life insurance policy. All of these gifts can be made easily. They are simple to explain and to understand, and minimal legal assistance is required. There are more complicated planned gift vehicles that require assistance, such as annuities and trusts. Your judicatory or denomination has an organization set up to help a donor make such gifts. For Episcopalians the organization is the Episcopal Church Foundation. Make your members aware of the various ways they can make planned gifts.

Asking involves general announcements and distribution of materials. It involves workshops or presentations to smaller groups in the parish. Asking also involves conversations with individuals that require both sensitivity and planning. You may be suggesting a particular kind of gift or a gift for a particular purpose. Think it through, and prepare a proposal you can leave with the person so he or she can discuss it with family or legal counsel. You are giving people an opportunity to help ensure the future health of something they love. Do your homework, and ask rightly. People frequently respond with exactly what you have asked for.

4. Encourage, where possible, unrestricted gifts.

I think donors put restrictions on their gifts for three reasons. First, the restriction might represent something they're passionate about. Second, the restriction might express a lack of trust in the present or future leadership. Third, the restriction might be an attempt to give with strings and maintain control. I am not opposed to restricted gifts, but I certainly favor gifts made without restrictions. Restrictions placed on gifts for the first reason are fine as long as you are willing to abide in perpetuity by the restriction. A demonstrated history of good financial leadership and asset management will reduce restrictions put on for the second reason. With regard to the third reason, you'll need to make sure that the restrictions are ones you can live with.

When donors put restrictions on gifts and you accept the gift, you are agreeing to abide by the restriction in perpetuity. If a living person gives you a gift restricted to a certain purpose, the donor can change the restriction. However, if the restriction is made by will or in a trust document, only the courts can change the restriction, so be sure that the restriction is worded in such a way that your successors two hundred years from now will still be able to observe the restriction. Here are some cautionary examples from my own experience. The Episcopal Diocese of New York holds one fund for the benefit of a parish that can be used only "for the purchase of Prayer Books, hymnals, red pew cushions and purple Altar hangings." Oh well, we live with that one. Another trust fund was set up over a century ago "to supplement the salaries of Clergymen paid less than $300 per year." After years of not being able to use the fund, the diocese petitioned the courts to amend the trust provisions so that we can use the fund to help "poorly paid clergy." The donor was unable to envision inflation, much less the ordination of women! Another donor in the 1890s stipulated that the funds had to be invested in railroad bonds — a better investment then than now.

We must resist the tyranny of the present when making and accepting restricted gifts. You'll want to make sure that there are no binding restrictions as to the investment vehicles permitted so you aren't locked into the present-day equivalent of railroad bonds. You'll want to make sure that the uses permitted will outlast the current generation. HIV/AIDS may well be curable in the future or eradicated altogether; you might not want a permanent restriction on a gift that the donor wants you to use now to help victims of that disease alone. Many bequests are made as legally unrestricted, but the will may say how the testator would like the gift to be used without making it a testamentary restriction. This approach allows the congregation voluntarily to observe the donor's desires without being legally bound.

5. Say "thank you."

It should hardly be necessary to say this, but it is. Most churches do not send out a letter thanking people after the pledge drive for making their annual pledges. On the whole we are not great at saying "thank you" to our members. Make sure you say thank you to the donor when you receive word of a planned gift before the donor's death. Maybe your judicatory has a way to recognize people who have let their parishes know that they've made a planned gift. The Stewardship Office of our diocese has established the Society of the Magi for this purpose. There are two reasons to thank people publicly, assuming the donors don't explicitly wish to be anonymous. First, it's nice to say "thank you" to someone who has given you something or promised to give you something. Second, of course, it encourages others to go and do likewise. Be sure to say "thank you" to the donor if you learn that the person has made provision for any kind of planned gift.

6. Celebrate them when they come.

Make sure people know when a planned gift has come, and by all means make sure everyone knows that you are doing with it what you said you would do with it.

Conclusion

St. Paul asked the Corinthians, "What do you have that you did not receive? And if you received it, why do you boast as if it were not a gift?" (1 Cor. 4:7b). Everything we have is a gift from above. If we think about what it has taken over two thousand years for us to be where we are, we will be deeply aware that we have any stature at all only because we are standing on the shoulders of all who have come before. Everything we are and everything we have are the gifts we've been given by God, by previous generations, and by those who have influenced and formed us.

It isn't too difficult to remember our debt to the past. All many of us have to do is to enter the buildings in which we worship, and a prayer of thanksgiving to God for those who have gone before swells in our hearts. The words of so many Bible passages and hymns that speak of our bonds with those now departed can easily catch in our throats and bring tears to our eyes.

It is somewhat more difficult to remember the future. However, all these gifts we've received from present and past generations are not in our permanent possession. They are in our keeping for a time, and at the end of that time we will pass them along. We are stewards of the gifts of God. During the time of our stewardship, we are accountable to one another. When God calls us home, we will give an account of our stewardship to God. And we will leave behind us for the next generation very clear evidence as to whether we remembered them as we did our work. They will know whether we took them into account or ignored them.

Our task as church leaders is the same as the task of every previous generation of church leaders: to continue to build on what we have inherited so that the next generation might have a more secure place to stand, so that they can continue to build. Certainly, hard work is indispensable; so is delight in the gifts God showers on us. Ambition, properly directed, has a place; so does a willingness to accept whatever role we are given to play. Planning and forethought are paramount; so is openness to what unfolds that might make alterations to the program we have designed.

The future is both the result of our efforts and what happens that is beyond our control. The future is both something we are moving toward and something that is moving toward us. Part of the mystery of the Creation is that God has given us an active part to play. We are not mere spectators, and we are not the passive victims of the cosmos. The results of our efforts may not always turn out as we imagined, but our efforts count. Our efforts, or our lack of them, will be part of the shape of the future others will live with.

My goals in these pages have been, first, to give you perhaps a new way to think about your role as a leader; second, to give you some practical tools you can use to play that role in a new way; and third and perhaps most important, to give you the necessary confidence to begin to play your role as a leader in a new way. You *can* make rational, prudent, and farsighted decisions about your property, your buildings, your money, and your members' support. These decisions are not the trivial concerns of the bean counters. These decisions are an integral part of the mission and ministry of the church, so people with a passionate vision about what the church can do are appropriately involved in making them. Passion alone, however, is not the basis on which to make these decisions. I think you need the approaches and attitudes I've tried to lay out.

What you decide about these matters today will affect for good or ill the future capacity of the church to fulfill its mission. So, as you are making those decisions, bear in mind that you are not alone, and *remember the future.*